THE DUTY TO CONSULT

THE DUTY TO CONSULT

NEW RELATIONSHIPS WITH ABORIGINAL PEOPLES

ooooo

DWIGHT G. NEWMAN

PURICH
PUBLISHING
LIMITED
SASKATOON, SK. CANADA

PURICH PUBLISHING LTD.
Box 23032, Market Mall Post Office, Saskatoon, SK, Canada, S7J 5H3
Tel: (306) 373-5311   Fax: (306) 373-5315   Email: purich@sasktel.net

Library and Archives Canada Cataloguing in Publication

Newman, Dwight
    The duty to consult : new relationships with Aboriginal peoples / Dwight
G. Newman.

(Purich's aboriginal issues series)
Includes index.
ISBN 978-1-895830-37-8

    1. Native peoples – Legal status, laws, etc. – Canada. 2. Native peoples –
Canada – Government relations. 3. Native peoples – Canada – Claims.
4. Constitutional law – Canada – Cases. I. Title. II. Series: Purich's
aboriginal issues series

KE7709.N49 2009   342.7108'72   C2009-904810-8
KF8205.N49 2009

Edited, designed, and typeset by Donald Ward.
Cover design by Duncan Campbell.
Index by Ursula Acton.

Purich Publishing gratefully acknowledges the assistance of the Government of Canada through the Book Publishing Industry Development Program and the Government of Saskatchewan through the Creative Economy Entrepreneurial Fund for its publishing program.

Printed on 100 per cent post-consumer, recycled, ancient-forest-friendly paper.

Updates on important developments on the duty to consult
will be available on our website: www.purichpublishing.com.

ACKNOWLEDGEMENTS

ᴏᴏᴏᴏᴏ

Iᴛ ʜᴀs ʙᴇᴇɴ ᴀ ᴅᴇʟɪɢʜᴛ ᴛᴏ ᴡᴏʀᴋ with Karen Belstad and Don Purich at Purich Publishing throughout the process on this book. Their enthusiasm and guidance on the project from the outset was helpful, their patience with delays as I faced the full challenges of the project appreciated, and their careful substantive comments on the manuscript valuable. I am honoured to have had this book accepted to join their distinguished line of books on Aboriginal, legal, and western Canadian issues.

I very much appreciate the editorial efforts of Donald Ward, who has done much to make the book more accessible to a wider audience. The book should be read by lawyers, of course, but also by non-lawyers, and if there remain places where the general reader finds remaining tones of the less accessible sorts of legalese, it is despite great efforts on his part. I also thank Ursula Acton for her skilled copy editing and indexing of the book.

The book frankly would not exist without the enormous efforts of Danielle Schweitzer, who worked as my research assistant through a large part of the process. She gathered what no doubt seemed to her endless legal and policy documents, and she carried out some of the interviews and surveys of stakeholders. I thank her for her tireless efforts.

I thank those who spoke with us, responded to written questions, or provided information that helped to flesh out perspectives of stakeholders and be more attentive to concerns beyond the academic context. In addition to a number who asked to remain anonymous, I thank Eric Cline, Pierre Cloutier de Repentigny, Jamie Dickson, Jerry Harvey, Teresa Homik, Jason

Madden, Mitch McAdam, Liam Mooney, Andy Popko, Nick Schultz, and Danielle Yeager.

I also thank Amy Jo Scherman, who worked as my research assistant during some final phases of the project and who faced with enthusiasm the rather inglorious task of checking and tracking down citations.

I presented papers related to parts of the book at the University of Toronto Legal Theory Workshop in December 2008, at the Canadian Law and Society Association Midwinter Meeting at Saint Mary's University in Halifax in January 2009, and at the Western Canadian Emerging Legal Scholars Workshop at the University of Manitoba in May 2009. I am grateful for the opportunity for feedback on these occasions. For their comments and questions, I thank in particular Natasha Affolder, Annie Bunting, Brenda Gunn, Heather Heavin, Patrick Macklem, Jane McMillan, David Milward, Sophia Moreau, Ronalda Murphy, Debra Parkes, Denise Réaume, David Schneiderman, Brian Slattery, Mariana Valverde, and Stephen Waddams. For encouragement and suggestions concerning sources on other occasions, I also thank Paul Chartrand, James (Sa'ke'j) Youngblood Henderson, Celeste Hutchinson, Courtney Kirk, and John Whyte.

I thank the Social Sciences and Humanities Research Council (SSHRC) for Standard Research Grant funding that has supported my research program on "Theorizing Aboriginal Rights," from which this book is one product.

I thank my spouse, Simonne Horwitz, for her constant encouragement and support.

And, finally, I thank you, the reader, for your readiness to engage in thinking about this complex subject through this book. I welcome any feedback from you as well.

Dwight G. Newman
Saskatoon
July 2009

CONTENTS

PREFACE

ooooo

Recent Aboriginal law doctrine in Canada is largely concerned with elaborating the implications of the Aboriginal rights provision in s. 35 of the *Constitution Act, 1982.*[1] Most recently, this body of law has become increasingly dominated by the case law of a new doctrine: the duty to consult. This duty is of major public interest, making regular appearances in media reports and drawing large numbers of people to major discussions on the issue. A duty to consult roundtable held in Saskatoon in May 2008, for example, drew 440 people.[2] Duties of consultation have been recognized in certain contexts for a longer period — particularly as part of the justification test first set out in *R. v. Sparrow*[3] for infringements of Aboriginal rights protected by s. 35. Recent discussion, however, springs from a trilogy of cases in 2004 and 2005: the *Haida Nation* case,[4] the *Taku River Tlingit First Nation* case,[5] and the *Mikisew Cree First Nation* case.[6] These three cases have set Aboriginal rights in Canada, and Aboriginal/ non-Aboriginal relations, on a fundamentally different course than they were on before. At the same time, they have generated many questions and a great deal of uncertainty.

This book is an attempt to clarify the duty to consult as a constitutional duty,[7] to offer some approaches to understanding the developing case law at a deeper and more principled level, and to say something about possible future directions for the duty to consult in Canadian Aboriginal law. I hope this discussion will be of interest to those who want a better understanding of the duty to consult, and the opportunity to reflect on relevant developments in relation to it. The duty to consult has a fundamental importance for Aboriginal communities and organizations, governments, industry stakeholders — indeed, all Canadians. Yet, there has been surprisingly little written on the duty to consult,[8] and misunderstandings are widespread. Individual readers may find different paths through the book; I welcome that, although I would suggest that there is an overall narrative flow to the book and I would urge readers to consider that as well.

The book begins from the fact that the *Haida Nation* trilogy and subsequent cases depart from earlier case law in elaborating the existence of a duty to consult Aboriginal communities potentially affected by government decision-making prior to final proof of an Aboriginal rights or Aboriginal title claim.[9] Although this duty had begun to be recognized in some lower courts before the Supreme Court of Canada recognized it,[10] the bulk of discussion around any consultation duties prior to this trilogy was in the much more limited context of the rules on infringement of established s. 35 rights.[11] These cases have transformed the discourse of the duty to consult and fundamentally altered the steps that government agencies must take prior to making various decisions. In these cases, the Court also decided that the duty to consult is one owed specifically by governments,[12] not by third-party corporate stakeholders, as some prior case law had suggested.[13] This decision shapes the duty in particular ways, although it does not diminish the impact of the duty on corporate stakeholders, particularly in the context of resource developments in traditional Aboriginal territories.[14] These cases, along with subsequent lower court decisions and various groups' policy making, have shaped the modern form of the duty to consult.

The complex frameworks in which the duty to consult is under discussion have suggested a particular format for this book. In Chapter 1 I will turn to a fuller discussion of the duty to consult trilogy and the key holdings from those three cases — thus offering an introduction to the fundamental doctrinal content of the duty to consult — before turning to several possible theoretical approaches to understanding the duty to consult, given the main doctrinal features from the first sketch.

Chapters 2 and 3 examine the judicial doctrine of the duty to consult as developed in subsequent lower court case law. Chapter 4 explores the development of duty to consult policies by governments, corporate stakeholders, and Aboriginal communities, arguing that this policy making further fleshes out the law. Chapter 5 draws on international and comparative law to offer some possibilities concerning future development of the duty to consult. The book thus seeks to further understanding of the doctrine on both a principled level and in terms of a more detailed examination of its development in the nearly five years since the *Haida Nation* trilogy. I will argue that the detailed examination of doctrine, policy, and practice is essential for coming to terms with any theoretically oriented understandings of the duty to consult.

The duty to consult is of national importance for Canada in terms of the future directions of Aboriginal law and Aboriginal/non-Aboriginal relations. It is also of international importance as part of the ongoing development of systems to better protect the rights of Indigenous peoples. This book, then, is an act of scholarship relevant to those national and international contexts, but at the same time it is a work deeply rooted in place. Although the book discusses case law from across Canada, it would be confusing to write as if the duty to consult affected all parts of the country in the same way. The demographics of Canada and the location of our larger resource industries make this book particularly rooted in and relevant to a Western Canadian demographic and developmental context.

The book has benefited from discussions with a number of stakeholders affected by the duty to consult and hopefully is more richly responsive to the relevance of the doctrine as a result. The stakeholders contacted have been from Western Canada, and the examples arising relate particularly to these contexts. This should not make the book any less relevant to those who live elsewhere, but make it richer for all.

This book discusses legal developments up to June 2009, thus describing developments in the close to five years since the *Haida Nation* judgment. At this writing, one major appeal the Supreme Court has agreed to consider is in the *Little Salmon/Carmacks* case from the Yukon Court of Appeal. Leave has recently been sought in the *Carrier Sekani* case from the British Columbia Court of Appeal, but the Supreme Court has not yet decided whether to hear an appeal in that case. There will obviously be doctrinal and policy developments in the years ahead, but the book seeks to get at the underlying principles in a manner that will hopefully endure over time.

In addition, I will be maintaining over the coming years a succinct summary of the most significant doctrinal and policy developments that can be read as a complement to the book and will appear on the publisher's website: www.purichpublishing.com.

ONE

ooooo

DOCTRINE AND THEORY

1.1 The Supreme Court Trilogy

Any discussion of the duty to consult in Canadian law must start with
the trilogy of cases that have transformed the field of discourse, particularly the *Haida Nation* decision, in which Chief Justice McLachlin set out
the fundamental terms of the doctrine.[1] The issue was the government's
replacement and transfer of a tree farm license to Weyerhaeuser, a large
forestry corporation. The Court held that the government ought to have
consulted the Haida Nation prior to these actions, as the Crown is bound
to act honourably in its relations with Aboriginal peoples. According to
the Supreme Court, this duty to consult arose even prior to a final proof of
a claim in the courts.[2]

It was precisely because the final shape of Aboriginal rights and title
had not yet been established that it was important for governments to
consult with the Aboriginal community so as not to affect their interests
detrimentally during the process of proving and resolving a claim. A legal duty to consult, wrote McLachlin C.J.C., "arises when the Crown has
knowledge, real or constructive, of the potential existence of the Aboriginal right or title and contemplates conduct that might adversely affect it."[3]
The content was to be defined based on a spectrum that takes into account
the strength of the claim and the seriousness of the potential adverse im-

pact on the right or title claimed.[4] Contrary to the conclusion of the Court of Appeal in the case, the Supreme Court of Canada held that the duty is one owed by the Crown only, due to its duties of honour, and not by third parties such as the forestry company.[5]

In *Haida Nation*, the impact of forestry on the Haida was serious, and the government had not consulted the community beforehand. The Supreme Court concluded that it had breached its duties and needed to consider significant accommodation.[6] In the companion case, *Taku River Tlingit First Nation*,[7] the Supreme Court ultimately concluded that the government had met the consultation requirements through an environmental assessment.[8] The case arose from a mining company's application to reopen an old mine in northwestern British Columbia; the company hoped to build a 160-km road to the mine through traditional Taku River Tlingit territory. The Tlingit raised concerns about the possible impacts on wildlife and other traditional uses, as well as their title claim. Although the potentially serious impacts implied some depth to the consultation,[9] there was a significant consideration of Aboriginal claims, including strategies on wildlife migration and the management and closure of the road. The court concluded that the government had met its duty.[10]

The *Mikisew Cree* case[11] extended this doctrine to treaty rights, subject to appropriate modifications.[12] The case arose following protests by the Mikisew Cree against the location of a winter road near their reserve on Treaty 8 lands in northern Alberta. The Mikisew Cree argued that this road would affect their traditional lifestyle because it crossed a number of trap lines and hunting grounds.[13] Where the Minister planned to "take up" lands under the treaty for the purpose of this road, the Supreme Court of Canada held that there was an obligation to consult in order to ensure that there was an honourable process in the "taking up" of these lands.[14] In this case, there had not been adequate consultation, and Justice Binnie's judgment sent the Crown back to deal with the project in light of the reasons elaborated in the judgment.[15] The duty to consult thus arises in relation to government actions that have potential impacts on treaty rights.[16] Obviously, what is known to the government in terms of the content of the right involved is more substantial in the context of treaty rights, thus rendering parts of the basic test less relevant.[17] Subject to the resulting modification, however, the duty to consult arises in the context of treaty rights on an approach parallel to that in the Aboriginal rights or title context.[18]

In these cases, the Supreme Court established a new legal doctrine — indeed, a new realm of Aboriginal law. What began with a simple tree farm license led to the need to understand a new legal framework in relation to Aboriginal rights, title, and treaty rights. This book seeks to offer readers an understanding of this area by going beyond the basics of the Supreme Court of Canada's three initial cases.

1.2 Understanding the Duty to Consult

The rights recognized and affirmed by s. 35 of the *Constitution Act, 1982* — which now include the duty to consult — are not specified by the written text of the Constitution. In some senses, then, the definition of s. 35 rights has been left to negotiations and to the courts. This is not owing to a lack of content to s. 35. Indeed, s. 35 merely "recognized and affirmed" rights that existed prior to European settlement and had, in many respects, ongoing status in the common law, even if not always effectively recognized.[19] However, uncertainties around the form and scope of these pre-existing rights, combined with the complex cross-cultural interaction of concepts,[20] have given rise to ongoing instability in Canada's constitutional law regarding Aboriginal rights, with concepts sometimes shifting rapidly in the space of a few years.[21]

This lack of stability is not surprising in constitutional law. In determining what a limited set of cases mean in the context of a case before the court, judges will consider the underlying meaning of the constitutional norms at issue, often in terms of the underlying theoretical scope of the concepts and a normative conception of the rights. So, for instance, a judge confronting an innovative factual case concerned with freedom of expression will consider not only the direct application of prior case law but also the underlying normative conceptualization of freedom of expression that this case law embodies. This is not to say that the judge has any duty other than to apply the law; it is, rather, to say that the content of the law is rich with meaning and a judge must work with this. There is, of course, a much longer-standing and larger body of normative analysis on the meaning of concepts such as freedom of expression than on the complex intersocietal concepts arising in the s. 35 context, which gives rise to ongoing challenges in applying the section in a consistent and principled manner. Judges are developing the body of thought in this area in the complex context of cross-cultural legal, normative, and political encounters.

An important question is that of on what normative conceptualizations of the duty to consult judges or others needing to interpret the law are to draw when faced with a novel legal question in a factual context unlike those that have come before. In such cases, judges must consider not just the determinate rules from prior cases but also the broader principles that these rules embody and instantiate.[22] Only by developing, with appropriate prudence and modesty, a broader theory of the law is it possible to address previously unanswered questions within the law.

One might suggest that the judges, in the duty to consult context, simply draw on a long-standing concept of the "honour of the Crown,"[23] but this does not displace the need to develop a broader theoretical account of the duty to consult in order to understand it. The early doctrinal foundations of the "honour of the Crown" consist of a concept that gave rise to a principle of interpretation that Crown grants should be interpreted in a manner such that they were not void.[24] Without further development of the concept, this doctrine has no immediate application in the context of the duty to consult. To understand the duty to consult, it is necessary to probe potentially deeper theoretical accounts. It would be imprudent to characterize the duty to consult before a careful analysis of the existing jurisprudence, but it is also important to set out some possibilities in order that one can consider them carefully as one proceeds through the more doctrinal discussion.

1.3 Theoretical Approaches to the Duty to Consult

To understand the duty to consult doctrine in a deeper sense, then, it is valuable to go behind the judgments to the more fundamental interests or principles the duty to consult furthers. Doing so provides a set of possible lenses for looking at the case law and evaluating each case as to how successfully it advances the doctrine's underlying purposes. It also enables an estimation of likely future directions of the duty. Particularly in the case of areas of law that are not fully defined by existing determinations of legal doctrine — such as in the context of Aboriginal rights protected by s. 35 of the Constitution — there is both a need to refer to existing doctrine and a need to go to the theoretical foundations of these areas to understand the law and its future development.

In terms of the basic doctrine from the Supreme Court of Canada's initial trilogy, to begin to distinguish among the fit of different theories of the doctrine, it is worth noting five fundamental components of the duty to consult as developed in those cases:

1) the duty to consult arises prior to proof of an Aboriginal rights or title claim or in the context of uncertain effects on a treaty right;[25]

2) the duty to consult is triggered relatively easily, based on a minimal level of knowledge on the part of the Crown concerning a possible claim with which government action potentially interferes;[26]

3) the strength or scope of the duty to consult in particular circumstances lies along a spectrum of possibilities, with a richer consultation requirement arising from a stronger *prima facie* Aboriginal claim and/or a more serious impact on the underlying Aboriginal right or treaty right;[27]

4) within this spectrum, the duty ranges from a minimal notice requirement to a duty to carry out some degree of accommodation of the Aboriginal interests, but it does not include an Aboriginal veto power over any particular decision;[28] and

5) failure to meet a duty to consult can lead to a range of remedies, from an injunction against a particular government action altogether (or, in some instance, damages) but more commonly an order to carry out the consultation prior to proceeding.[29]

The most commonly advanced theoretical foundation for the duty to consult doctrine is that provided by the Court itself as an explanation of the grounding of the doctrine, with McLachlin C.J.C. explaining in *Haida Nation* that the "government's duty to consult with Aboriginal peoples and accommodate their interests is grounded in the honour of the Crown."[30] Her discussion of the honour of the Crown encompasses, in adjacent text, a discussion of the idea that the honour of the Crown also embodies such related principles as that the Crown should not engage in "sharp dealing" in making or interpreting treaties,[31] potentially suggesting a somewhat attenuated version of the content of the honour at stake.

Nonetheless, there is a legal obligation on governments arising from the principle that the Crown must act in accordance with a particular virtue —

namely, honour. The concept of the Crown, of course, is symbolic, with the underlying foundation amounting to a claim that a settler people in an on-going encounter with Indigenous peoples must deal honourably with them and, more generally, act in accordance with the virtue of honour.

This theoretical approach can fit readily into some of the features of the duty to consult doctrine. It fits easily enough with the claim that governments must consult with Aboriginal peoples about unproven claims, for the prospect of the undermining of an Aboriginal right while it is stalled in litigation or negotiation would be dishonourable. Similarly, the easy triggering of the duty to consult fits with a plausible conception of honour. Our conception of honour needs to be reasonably fulsome, for if we acknowledge that one of its central components is a prohibition against sharp dealing, sharp dealing on the application of the concept itself cannot be permitted. On this standard, though, the spectrum of duties potentially embraced by the duty to consult in particular circumstances becomes more difficult to justify. To suppose that it is stronger in some circumstances and weaker in others does not sit easily with an effort to ensure that (honourable) dealing is above reproach. Indeed, it arguably appears to contain more of a weighing of costs and benefits than any conceptions of honour will contain.

This realization leads us directly to a second possible theoretical approach to the duty to consult, one to which the Court adverts in *Haida Nation*, although less explicitly. Prior to discussing the duty to consult in *Haida Nation*, the Court considered first whether to grant an interlocutory injunction until there was a resolution of the Aboriginal rights case. Chief Justice McLachlin dismissed the possibility:

> An interlocutory injunction over such a long period of time might work unnecessary prejudice and may diminish incentives on the part of the successful party to compromise. While Aboriginal claims can be and are pursued through litigation, negotiation is a preferable way of reconciling state and Aboriginal interests. For all these reasons, interlocutory injunctions may fail to adequately take account of Aboriginal interests prior to their final determination.[32]

This dismissal is part of the grounding for the duty to consult doctrine that the Court elaborates later in the judgment, implicitly constituting part of the justification for this latter doctrine. This justification, then, is implicitly that the duty to consult doctrine — as compared to an approach founded on interlocutory injunctions during litigation or negotiation — fosters appropriate incentives for negotiation and is thus preferable on the grounds of what will promote the best negotiation processes between Aboriginal and non-Aboriginal communities, thus calling for attention to a certain kind of consequence of the doctrinal framework.

In one sense, this theoretical explanation of the doctrine wo   uld assert the responsibility of the courts to cast the "shadow of the law" — which is sometimes described as what shape it puts on negotiation contexts[33] — to facilitate something desirable within the negotiation processes. This kind of explanation, of course, does not have to say that the proper analysis of the duty to consult in specific circumstances is that which facilitates the best negotiation process or outcome in those particular circumstances. The courts' rationale for promoting negotiation in the Aboriginal law context — a not infrequently expressed preference[34] — is, in part, that they lack significant information that the parties can best bring to bear on a particular Aboriginal rights negotiation.[35] Lacking full information about particular circumstances and promoting negotiation for precisely this reason, the courts might then easily promote appropriate negotiation through a structuring of such contexts that creates appropriate incentives for the parties themselves.

This theoretical approach to the duty to consult fits more readily with the notion of a spectrum. The structuring of negotiation will be dependent on the circumstances that give rise to claims for greater or lesser bargaining power by the different parties. It is appropriate that Aboriginal communities with relatively stronger *prima facie* claims or whose claims are more seriously affected have greater power in the relevant negotiation processes. This theoretical approach thus more readily explains the spectrum analysis within the duty to consult.

It can be argued, however, that it sits less easily with the notion of an easy triggering of the duty to consult. On this theoretical approach, the notion of the spectrum within the duty to consult is one advancing a structuring of negotiations in accordance with relevant moral considerations. An Aboriginal rights claim of little *prima facie* strength in the context of a near-trivial impact on the community would arguably not give rise to a moral reason to create any bargaining power at all for the Aboriginal community, yet the duty to consult doctrine would nonetheless create some rights, if only at a minimal level.[36]

Perhaps more significantly, a theoretical approach based on these kinds of result-oriented considerations would speak to an element that is not present in the duty to consult — namely, a limitation of the duty to consult in some circumstances where limitations would be justified on an appropriate cost-benefit analysis. (The argument for a less easy triggering of the duty is actually a special case of this broader point.) If there were specifiable circumstances in which the introduction of a duty to consult would skew negotiations in a manner that promoted inefficiency, a results-oriented account of the doctrine would lean toward taking account of these circumstances in the form of further limits on the doctrine. So, for example, circumstances in which governments wished to develop certain lands for significant economic development purposes would, on this account, reasonably give rise to a more attenuated duty to consult in relation to proposed government activities on those lands.

A third theoretical approach to the duty to consult would see it as a doctrine promoting "reconciliation" — itself a complex and contested concept in Aboriginal law, as I have discussed elsewhere,[37] but one not easily described as a result because it is often seen more in terms of a process. This theoretical approach would, like the others, find some basis in the text of the *Haida Nation* judgment:

> Honourable negotiation implies a duty to consult with Aboriginal claimants and conclude an honourable agreement reflecting the claimants' inherent rights. But proving rights may take time, sometimes a very long time. In the meantime, how are the interests under discussion to be treated? Underlying this question is the need to reconcile prior Aboriginal occupation of the land with the reality of Crown sovereignty. Is the Crown, under the aegis of its asserted sovereignty, entitled to use the resources at issue as it chooses, pending proof and resolution of the Aboriginal claim? Or must it adjust its conduct to reflect the as yet unresolved rights claimed by the Aboriginal claimants?[38]

Within this account, then, the duty to consult is posited as a doctrine encapsulating a just reconciliation between the Crown and Aboriginal peoples in the context of unproven claims.[39] The duty to consult is an adjustment of government conduct to reflect unresolved claims, as part of a reconciliation of prior Aboriginal occupation and current Crown sovereignty.

Specific formulations of this account might potentially collapse into one of the other accounts,[40] but this account could be described as related to a more generalized account of just relations among communities in the context of unresolved claims among those communities, or as striking a sort of balance between rights claims in the context of uncertainties about those claims. It could conceivably be situated within broader accounts of just relations between communities or within broader accounts related to rights conflicts. There would thus clearly be more that one could develop within this account, for several possible versions are implicit within it. Indeed, without that further development, it faces a danger of being able to provide relatively limited guidance on implications for the doctrine. That said, something like this will obviously fit with some elements of the doctrine, with it following reasonably that an account of just relations between and among communities and/or rights conflicts between them will properly become involved in analysis based on a relatively low standard for the triggering of the duty to consult, and that the scope of the duty that mediates between the communities will then be adjusted to the circumstances of the relationship in the context of a particular rights conflict. To say this, however, is to submerge a larger set of questions concerning the details of this theoretical account that do not surface as easily from the text itself. For present purposes, however, I will leave it at that and say that some such account could plausibly emerge in a more detailed form.

A fourth possible theoretical approach to the duty to consult, different yet again, would see the judicial development of a duty to consult as exemplifying and fostering what some would assert to be a broader normative commitment of Aboriginal law — namely, that it promote what Slattery terms a "generative constitutional order."[41] Such a theoretical approach would, as Slattery describes it, see "section 35 as serving a dynamic and not simply static function."[42] Parts of the *Haida Nation* judgment appear to situate the duty to consult within this kind of dynamic process:

> the duty to consult and accommodate is part of a process of fair dealing and reconciliation that begins with the assertion of sovereignty and continues beyond formal claims resolution. Reconciliation is not a final legal remedy in the usual sense. Rather it is a process flowing from rights guaranteed by s. 35(1). . . .[43]

This account of the duty to consult would see it as promoting an ongoing process of reconciliation. Concerned with an ethic of ongoing relationships, it would fit with some elements of the doctrine, notably the circumstances in which it arises and the preference for remedies for violations that promote ongoing negotiations. This account would also ground an unlimited doctrine, one not completed at any particular moment in the context of an ongoing relationship. However, the notion of the spectrum within the duty to consult doctrine is that a duty to consult can in some circumstances be successfully fulfilled without an ongoing course of consultations. So, again, there are ways in which this possible foundation of the duty to consult doctrine fits more and less well.

Each of these theories more readily fits some aspects of the doctrine than others. The obvious implication is that each, if adopted as a more definitive theoretical foundation, would push elements of the doctrine in different directions. To take one example in the elements already under discussion, an honour-oriented account would minimize the role of the spectrum analysis within the doctrine, whereas a results-oriented account would tend to expand it.

The different theoretical accounts will have different implications, as well, for questions not explicitly addressed thus far. Initial pronouncements on the modern duty to consult have tended to limit its application explicitly to Crown decisions and, implicitly, decisions concerning Crown lands. Lower court case law, more recently, has reawakened questions about the implications of the duty to consult for decisions related to privately owned lands, in light of suggestions in some of this lower court case law that there remains more to be said about the implications of Aboriginal title for privately owned lands.[44] The different theoretical approaches to the duty to consult potentially lead in significantly different directions on such questions. At the very least, they lead to entirely different analyses; given that, it might be surprising if they led to the same outcomes. An open-ended fostering of a generative constitutional order would presumably be favourable toward an expansion of the generative scope of the constitutional order. An approach concerned with reconciliation might look to the effects of opening such questions on prospects for reconciliation. A results-oriented account would look to the effects on negotiation contexts, likely having concerns with the uncertainties created for private landowners. An honour-oriented account would look to the overall honour of Canada's dealings with Aboriginal peoples, and would potentially be more sympathetic to the prospect of this development. These descriptions of likely attitudes are, of course, tentative, in that one could pursue significantly more work within each of these accounts to flesh out the account and its implications for this scenario. But they are sufficient to reinforce the likelihood that these different underlying accounts lead in different directions on controversial questions concerning the duty to consult.

The potential instability in the law relative to different theoretical underpinnings for it speaks to one reason we might have for seeking a more definitive theoretical account of the duty to consult doctrine. Although theoretical argument has been a major driver in Supreme Court of Canada case law on Aboriginal rights, particularly in the context of s. 35, in many different s. 35 contexts, there are these remaining sorts of uncertainties in relation to theoretical underpinnings, and these uncertainties may be a possible explanation of some of the kinds of dramatic shifts we have seen in some areas of Aboriginal law through the post-1982 period. In some senses, then, the particular example of theorizing the duty to consult presents a subset of the challenges in theorizing Aboriginal law more generally.

It is important to recognize the presence in the duty to consult case law of several distinct theoretical foundations for the doctrine, some of the inconsistencies between them and their implications, and some of the interactions with the more general domain of theorizing Aboriginal law. Coming closer to answers on the theoretical foundation for the duty to consult will depend on further discussion of more detailed elements of the doctrine, more examples of its applications by lower courts that are actually putting it in practice, and the development of practices and policies by various stakeholders.

TWO

ooooo

LEGAL PARAMETERS
OF THE DUTY TO CONSULT

2.1 Introduction

The Supreme Court of Canada's case law is explicit that its consideration of the duty to consult has been partial and is to leave room for development of the doctrine by the lower courts. As Chief Justice McLachlin described it in *Haida Nation*,

> This case is the first of its kind to reach this Court. Our task is the modest one of establishing a general framework for the duty to consult and accommodate . . . before Aboriginal title or rights have been decided. As this framework is applied, courts, in the age-old tradition of the common law, will be called on to fill in the details of the duty to consult and accommodate.[1]

Justice Donald of the British Columbia Court of Appeal has recognized the lower courts' role in taking up this task, describing a recent judgment as pertaining to "one of those cases foreseen by the Supreme Court of Canada . . . where the broad general principles of the Crown's duty to consult and, if necessary, accommodate Aboriginal interests are to be applied to a concrete set of circumstances."[2] Justice Slatter of the Alberta Court of Appeal puts it more colourfully in stating that the "exact content of the duty to consult is in its formative stages, and is still being hammered out on the anvils of justice."[3]

Given the Supreme Court's acknowledgement of the ongoing development of the duty to consult in the lower courts, it is the combination of the judgments of the Supreme Court of Canada together with the decisions of lower courts seeking to work with the duty to consult in more applied contexts that actually defines the legal shape of the duty. These lower court judgments are making many details clearer, but they are also complicating some issues on which disagreement is emerging or on which courts are choosing not to answer particular points. Nonetheless, to come to an understanding of the duty to consult, there is no alternative to grappling with the case law. My aspiration is to fit the case law as well as possible into a principled framework, seeking to integrate rather than to divide. It is important to note that there will be different issues in different provinces, with live Aboriginal title issues being vastly more widespread in British Columbia than elsewhere, and the duty to consult case law thus appearing to develop differently when the differences actually arise at least partly from differences in the underlying factual circumstances. In any case, the effort to integrate the law into more principled frameworks hopefully has potential.

This chapter examines, in a sense, the place of the duty to consult within the Canadian legal order, framed in terms of three questions:

1) When does a duty to consult arise?

2) What stakeholders are involved in a consultation?

3) When is consultation and accommodation subject to review by the courts?

In Chapter 3, I will explore the implications of the case law for the content of the duty to consult in particular circumstances.

2.2 Triggering the Duty to Consult

The duty to consult becomes legally relevant based on certain "triggering conditions." These triggering conditions denote a set of threshold requirements that must be met before any duty to consult arises in a particular circumstance. In the absence of these triggering conditions, there is no duty to consult.[4] Although one should not push these analogies too far, the question of whether a duty to consult is triggered parallels that of whether a *Charter* right is engaged. Before we examine if there has been a breach of a *Charter* right or the Crown has conducted itself in a manner keeping with its duty to consult, we need to know that a particular fact situation raises the question in the first place. Chief Justice McLachlin offers the leading statement of the test in the *Haida Nation* case:

> [W]hen precisely does a duty to consult arise? The foundation of the duty in the Crown's honour and the goal of reconciliation suggest that the duty arises when the Crown has knowledge, real or constructive, of the potential existence of the Aboriginal right or title and contemplates conduct that might adversely affect it.[5]

Justice Binnie clarifies in *Mikisew Cree* that the same principle applies in the context of treaty rights.[6]

The duty to consult, then, is triggered based on a knowledge element and an adverse effect element. The knowledge element is met when the Crown has actual or constructive knowledge of a potential Aboriginal rights or title claim or of an Aboriginal claim under a treaty. The adverse effect element is met when the Crown contemplates conduct that might adversely affect Aboriginal title, an Aboriginal right, or a treaty right. This latter component contains, in turn, two questions: when is there an "adverse effect," and what is the nature of the conduct "contemplated" by the Crown?

2.2(a) Knowledge of the Aboriginal Title, Right, or Treaty Right

In terms of the knowledge element, the test as expressed in *Haida Nation* does not contemplate a duty to consult where the government could not possibly have formed an idea of the claimed right,[7] but the test does contemplate a duty even where there is uncertainty about a claim.[8] According to this test, uncertainty about a claim may affect the scope of the duty to consult in particular circumstances, but it does not fundamentally undermine the existence of the duty.[9]

The concept of actual knowledge of an Aboriginal title claim is the most straightforward scenario in terms of triggering the duty to consult. Where an Aboriginal title claim has been either filed in court or been claimed in the context of negotiations with government, the Crown will have actual knowledge of it. Constructive knowledge of an Aboriginal title claim is slightly more complicated. Where, for example, certain lands are known or reasonably suspected to have been traditionally occupied by an Aboriginal community, the Crown could be deemed to have constructive knowledge of an Aboriginal title claim in respect of such lands.[10]

This triggering of the duty to consult will have significant implications in areas of the country with unresolved Aboriginal title issues, particularly in British Columbia. However, given the similarity of Aboriginal reserve land to Aboriginal title land, affirmed by the Supreme Court of Canada in *Osoyoos Indian Band*,[11] one may reasonably infer that possible effects on reserve lands will similarly trigger the duty to consult,[12] extending the implications across the country.

The duty to consult, however, is not triggered only by Aboriginal title claims. The doctrine, as expressed in *Haida Nation*, also refers to the triggering of the duty to consult by Aboriginal rights claims. This has a much broader potential than one confined to the context of title claims. An Aboriginal title claim arises only in the context of identifiable lands under a claim of Aboriginal title. An Aboriginal rights claim arises when an Aboriginal pre-contact practice may continue in the form of a modern-day Aboriginal right.[13]

A basic reading of the Supreme Court of Canada's jurisprudence on the duty to consult would suggest that the duty to consult would be triggered in a wide variety of circumstances where the government was actually or constructively aware of an Aboriginal rights claim that could be adversely affected by its contemplated action. Given the sheer diversity of possible Aboriginal rights claims, this dimension of the test raises some complex issues in terms of the scope of the circumstances in which governments might be considered to have knowledge of a potential Aboriginal rights claim. In some cases that have been litigated on the duty to consult, for example, Aboriginal communities have argued that they should be consulted in respect of any government action affecting some dimension of their claimed scope of Aboriginal self-government.[14] This claim has been met by case law that somewhat attenuates the broad approach on the knowledge element to which the initial Supreme Court of Canada cases seem to have been inclined.

An additional complexity here is that the scope of the duty to consult is dependent on the current state of the law on the scope of the Aboriginal rights that undergird a duty to consult in particular circumstances. The Supreme Court of Canada's initial statement of the Aboriginal rights test in *Van der Peet*[15] has been subject to some important critiques, with the Court recently taking some of them into consideration in its tweaking of the *Van der Peet* test in *Sappier* and *Gray*.[16] Thus, one might think there could be possibilities for the Aboriginal rights test to be subject to modification over time in a process of gradual legal change. Ironically, the addition of the duty to consult to the jurisprudence might actually discourage such change. Any future shift in the test for Aboriginal rights would also shift the duty to consult, and to the extent that any shifts in the Aboriginal rights test became foreseeable, the Crown would implicitly have constructive knowledge of potential Aboriginal rights claims under a modified law even before the law changed. So, any suggestions of anything other than reasonably complete stability in the Aboriginal rights test would open new applications of the duty to consult even before these changes could be debated and subjected to adjudication. The effects of suggestions of instability in the Aboriginal rights test thus become a reason against permitting any perception of possible changes in the law in this area. The development of the duty to consult, then, becomes a factor that may discourage the development of other Aboriginal rights jurisprudence. This obviously raises matters that could be subjected to further discussion, but the most that can be said here is to raise the possibility and watch the developing Aboriginal rights case law in the years ahead to see whether it gives any indications of this consequence.

Finally, Crown knowledge of a treaty right that its conduct may adversely affect also triggers the duty to consult. There seems little potential for argument that the Crown was actually and constructively unaware of a particular treaty rights claim, for the Crown is a treaty rights partner in every instance. As Justice Binnie puts it in *Mikisew Cree*, "In the case of a treaty the Crown, as a party, will always have notice of its contents."[17] However, the claims made under a particular treaty, as well as claims as to the correct interpretation of a treaty, will sometimes be more complex. Although the treaty context will significantly modify the approach to the question of whether a duty to consult is triggered,[18] there will continue to be claims made as to treaty rights that turn out in fact not to engage the duty to consult.[19]

The test for the triggering of the duty to consult offered in *Haida Nation* contemplates a duty even in the face of significant uncertainty about a particular Aboriginal title or Aboriginal rights claim. As described by McLachlin C.J.C.,

> There is a distinction between knowledge sufficient to trigger a duty to consult and, if appropriate, accommodate, and the content or scope of the duty in a particular case. Knowledge of a credible but unproven claim suffices to trigger a duty to consult and accommodate. The content of the duty, however, varies with the circumstances, as discussed more fully below. A dubious or peripheral claim may attract a mere duty of notice, while a stronger claim may attract more stringent duties. The law is capable of differentiating between tenuous claims, claims possessing a strong *prima facie* case, and established claims. Parties can assess these matters, and if they cannot agree, tribunals and courts can assist. Difficulties associated with the absence of proof and definition of claims are addressed by assigning appropriate content to the duty, not by denying the existence of a duty.[20]

Justice Binnie implicitly adopts the same statement for the treaty context in *Mikisew Cree*.[21] In all the different contexts, then, the Supreme Court appears to commend an approach to the knowledge element in the triggering of the duty to consult that considers it easily met, with adjustment for the relative strength or weakness of the elements underpinning the duty in particular circumstances playing out in the content of the duty in those circumstances.

Lower courts engaged with duty to consult situations since the Supreme Court's early pronouncements have been more ready to add internal limits to the circumstances in which the duty is triggered, thus offering a somewhat more tempered version of the law on the duty to consult. In the context of the knowledge requirement, lower courts have recognized more possibility of a lack of evidence for an Aboriginal title or right to give rise to a non-triggering of the duty to consult. In *Native Council of Nova Scotia* v. *Canada*,[22] the Federal Court of Canada, in a judgment affirmed on the same grounds by the Federal Court of Appeal,[23] held that the offering of limited evidence to the Court of a claimed Aboriginal right meant that the duty to consult was not engaged. Similarly, in *Ahousaht Indian Band* v. *Canada (Minister of Fisheries & Oceans)*,[24] the Federal Court of Appeal emphasized that the proof submitted of an Aboriginal right giving rise to consultation requirements needed to go beyond "mere submissions" to meaningful evidence.[25] That said, courts have recognized that it would not be reasonable to demand more than a "credible claim."[26]

Nonetheless, where the government could meaningfully form an idea of there being Aboriginal title, an Aboriginal right, or a treaty right, this element of the test will be satisfied.

2.2(b) Adverse Effect Element of the Triggering Test

Knowledge of the existence of Aboriginal title claims, Aboriginal rights claims, and treaty rights claims grounds the duty to consult in general terms. However, for there to be a duty to consult in particular circumstances, the knowledge of a particular title or rights claims must be linked to the contemplation of government action that, on the Supreme Court of Canada's description, "might adversely affect it."[27] Although this phrase does not appear to call for an especially stringent test but for a reasonably easy triggering of a duty to consult, it has nonetheless given rise in lower courts' jurisprudence to some internal limits on when the duty to consult is triggered.

The fact that there would be internal limits is appropriate. The Supreme Court's terminology reflects a view of there being some limits on the effects considered to give rise to a duty to consult, for it requires not just any effect but a specifically detrimental effect, making it appropriate to evaluate the effects in a particular instance.

Some of the suggested internal limits propose that the duty to consult not be triggered where there is a relatively minimal adverse effect. For example, the British Columbia Court of Appeal in *Douglas*[28] held that a duty to consult was not triggered by a policy change that had "no appreciable adverse effect on the First Nations' ability to exercise their Aboriginal right."[29] This case was in the context of a limitation on an established right — specifically, whether the development of certain rules on a sport fishery required further consultation after there had been consultation with Aboriginal communities about an overall fisheries strategy — with the Court deciding that the consultation about the overall strategy was adequate without further discussion. The case nonetheless helps us interpret the triggering standard. The Court cited this "no appreciable effect" standard back to *Haida Nation*'s test on adverse effect,[30] although it obviously adds a gloss to the test in that it begins to suggest that one can look to how "appreciable" any adverse effect is. The Alberta Court of Appeal in

Lefthand would seemingly have imposed even more substantial limits.[31] Slatter J.A.'s judgment would recognize a duty to consult only where a *prima facie* breach of an Aboriginal or treaty right was established,[32] and would recognize a *prima facie* breach only where the accused could show some "unreasonableness, hardship, or interference" resulting to a preferred means of exercising the right.[33] Other judgments in the case, notably that of Conrad J.A., appear in some respects to be going back to pre-*Haida Nation* analysis, so the case may not fully reflect an interpretation of the modern duty. But it nonetheless suggests the view of some appellate courts that there needs to be a larger set of internal limits on the triggering test for a duty to consult.

The Supreme Court's stated purpose in *Haida Nation* was to recognize that actions affecting unproven Aboriginal title or rights or treaty rights can have irreversible effects that are not in keeping with the honour of the Crown.[34] To the extent that case law in the lower courts goes too far in setting new standards of proof of *prima facie* breaches, it is inconsistent with the main thrust of the *Haida Nation* jurisprudence. To the extent that lower court case law recognizes that there needs to be a real adverse effect at issue before a duty to consult is triggered, however, it carries forward the duty to consult test. Although the Supreme Court seemingly offered an easily triggered duty, with scope for modification of the requirements in a specific context, the triggering of a duty to consult by every government action that could, through some remote process, have some minimal adverse effect on an Aboriginal right would set up an impractical scenario for government decision-making. To say this much is not to undermine the purposes of the duty to consult, but to make it workable and efficacious in furthering reconciliation processes. It is also appropriate to conclude, as the Federal Court of Appeal has, that a situation where a government action might affect an Aboriginal right, but only through a remote causal chain, does not trigger a duty to consult.[35]

Lower court case law further suggests that the government action at issue may also affect whether a duty to consult is triggered. Where a branch or level of government carries out a mandate established by another government, it may not trigger a duty to consult because any duty to consult would have arisen in respect of the initial decision to develop the mandate. Recognizing this concept brings together what might otherwise seem potentially unexplained decisions not to recognize a duty to consult. In a case concerning the decision of a prosecutor to go ahead with a case, the

Federal Court of Appeal has suggested that the principles of the separation of powers mean that the prosecutor is not under a duty to consult.[36] In a case concerning the actions of a municipal board carrying out land development, the Alberta Court of Appeal has suggested that a municipal entity is not expected to carry out a more extended consultation than that within the processes set out for it within its statutes.[37] The carrying out of an established mandate does not trigger a duty to consult, for the consultation should have occurred at the stage at which the mandate was being established.

According to some case law, the creation of legislation is also outside the application of the duty to consult. This is one of the conclusions of the Alberta Court of Queen's Bench in the *Tsuu T'ina* case,[38] in which it decided that the Minister's recommendation of and Cabinet's adoption of a water management plan had not breached any consultation requirement. The Court there followed what it conceived as one determination of the Alberta Court of Appeal decision in *Lefthand*,[39] in which the Alberta Court of Appeal held that there was no violation of duty to consult requirements in the Alberta government's establishment of a "bait ban." Interpreting the *Lefthand* decision is complicated because the Court split three ways. However, Slatter J.A.'s judgment does put forcefully the claim that legislative processes are not subject to the duty to consult; it would be "an unwarranted interference with the proper functioning of the House of Commons and the Provincial Legislatures to require that they engage in any particular processes prior to the passage of legislation."[40] Watson J.A. concurs,[41] thus making it the majority view of the Alberta Court of Appeal in this case.

Readers will have noted that the conclusions from the previous two paragraphs are inconsistent. In the one case, the argument is that a municipal governmental entity cannot carry out consultation, for any consultation ought to have occurred at the time these governmental entities were being established in a form that did not involve further consultation in carrying out various decisions. In the other case, the argument is that no consultation ought to take place at the legislative stage. Both restraints come from the Alberta Court of Appeal, but the reasoning for each is in tension with the other. The constraints on when duties to consult arise will obviously be subject to further discussion and development.

However these questions concerning other constraints are resolved, the primary context for the duty to consult is administrative decision-making by government that may have a real adverse effect. The precise triggering test may depend on the sort of right at issue. There are powerful arguments in the lower court case law that the reason for an apparently easy triggering test in the Supreme Court of Canada cases was partly motivated by the context of Aboriginal title that could be irreversibly affected. Where one is concerned with an Aboriginal right such that the government action could be reversed without lasting effect on that right, there is a stronger argument for a constitutional duty to consult not being triggered as readily.

2.2(c) Contemplated Government Conduct

The second component of the test implicitly contains a third element, which can be a further complicating factor.

The Supreme Court of Canada's case law does not delve meaningfully into an analysis of what level of contemplation is needed for particular government planning to trigger the duty to consult. In some situations, in which the duty to consult has significant relevance, the issue requires more detailed analysis. If the government issues a permit for exploratory steps that might move toward a larger project, but only if it turns out to be economically worthwhile, the question is whether the granting of a permit at the initial stage triggers the duty to consult, or if the duty to consult is triggered only when there is full consideration of the larger project.

The Federal Court in *Dene Tha' First Nation* v. *Canada*[42] takes a view of contemplated conduct that looks to a larger project that could reasonably be seen to flow from the current decision-making processes. Justice Phelan adopted this approach in the context of early decisions related to the construction of the MacKenzie Gas Pipeline, noting that the pipeline was not merely an idea in the heads of a few governmental officials but a plan with a road map toward the project,[43] and holding that this meant there should have been consultation from that earlier stage. The factual element of there being a definite longer-term plan present might make the case unique on its facts. But Phelan J.'s reasoning does seem to lend itself to a broader reading of the principle here. Justice Phelan cites back to what was really at stake with the tree farm licenses in *Haida Nation*,[44] arguing that the conduct contemplated in granting a tree farm license properly engaged the duty to consult not so much because of the specific license decision but because it involved "strategic planning for the utilization of the resource."[45]

Saskatchewan's system for mineral, oil, and gas dispositions provides an interesting example that, in terms of the practicalities, might weigh in the other direction.[46] For mineral rights, Saskatchewan's system continues to be based on staking — physical staking in the north and map-staking in the south — with the party staking and filing a claim with the Ministry of Energy and Resources gaining legal priority over all others in the rights to the minerals.[47] For oil and gas rights, a company confidentially requests that rights in a certain area be put for sale and the Province then puts them up for sale at quarterly auctions. The Ministry is now putting caveats in some land sale notices to alert prospective purchasers that duty to consult requirements may arise in the development of certain lands.[48] The Ministry has also taken the position that it can carry out the sale of oil and gas rights without consultation at that stage because Aboriginal interests would not be affected until there is an actual permit to develop those oil and gas rights, that then being the stage at which duty to consult requirements would arise.[49] Although there have been lawsuits threatened by some Aboriginal communities over the issue, this position does have a degree of significant practicality to it. Until an actual decision is under contemplation that has the potential to affect rights, the sale of oil and gas rights that might or might not be developed — depending on later decisions on various other issues — and that might be developed in a variety of ways, each having potentially different implications for Aboriginal interests, arguably cannot be considered to trigger the duty to consult with every Aboriginal community that might be affected in some future scenario after the issuance of further permits.

But thinking of the duty to consult in a permit-by-permit manner is inconsistent with the reasoning in the *Dene Tha'* case, and there is a possibility that such an approach could result in "death by a thousand cuts."[50] If an Aboriginal community does not realize the significance of each permit being issued as part of a larger project, it may not have a fair opportunity to respond to the effect of the overall project. Indeed, a permit-by-permit approach to consultation may be impractical and unworkable for all concerned,[51] since it will set in motion a process for each permit in a manner inconsistent with the goals of the duty to consult and creating delays and problems in the meantime. In some circumstances, it may be appropriate for the government to consult on a general strategy such that the duty to consult would not then be engaged by every decision along the way.[52] However, these matters must be decided contextually in the manner most appropriate to the issues at stake.

As part of its approach to consultation in particular circumstances, the government ought to consider in good faith whether a particular decision is inherently connected to a larger strategy or project in a manner other than exploring the possibility of that strategy or project. If so, it may be appropriate to consider consultation about the larger undertaking from the outset, or at least from whenever it crystallizes.

2.2(d) Summary on Triggering Test

The application of the triggering test is obviously far from simple. Where government departments are uncertain about whether their action triggers a duty to consult, the safer course may be to act as if it did and extend at least notice of the proposed action to potentially affected Aboriginal communities. After all, a failure to consult may provoke litigation that will cause delays in the government action. Moreover, there is an important rationale for some ease in the triggering of a duty to consult; in circumstances where an Aboriginal community will be able to add to the Crown understanding of the extent of impact of particular decisions, it may be valuable for the duty to be considered triggered simply in order to ensure that there is input from the Aboriginal community.[53]

Government departments need not consult in circumstances where there are overriding doubts about the Aboriginal title or right or treaty right. They need not consult in circumstances where there is no plausible adverse effect on an Aboriginal claim. They need not consult if they are not involved in the kinds of action that trigger a duty to consult. However, it is not always easy for government officials to make those determinations with certainty, which may support the notion that to avoid the risk of not consulting in circumstances where consultation should have occurred, where there is any argument for doing so and it is practical to do so, at least notice to Aboriginal communities should be extended. It would be impractical to consult on every governmental decision, though, so there is a need for good judgment in applying this principle.

There may be other exceptions as well. For example, there are judicial statements to the effect that, if urgent circumstances preclude consultation in a particular instance, this may mean that a duty to consult is not triggered.[54] Although any broad reading of such an exception would vitiate the purposes of the doctrine, any decision not to have such an exception would undermine the aims of the law as well. Thus, there may be additional exceptions in special circumstances, as guided by the purposes of the duty to consult doctrine.

2.3 Consultation Partners

The constitutional duty to consult is a duty owed by the Crown. One of the Supreme Court of Canada's decisions in the *Haida Nation* case was that the Court of Appeal's judgment that would have imposed the duty to consult on third parties was without legal foundation. Chief Justice McLachlin made clear that the Crown alone bears ultimate responsibility under the duty to consult:

> The Crown alone remains legally responsible for the consequences of its actions and interactions with third parties, that affect Aboriginal interests. The Crown may delegate procedural aspects of consultation to industry proponents seeking a particular development; this is not infrequently done in environmental assessments. Similarly, the terms of T.F.L. 39 mandated Weyerhaeuser to specify measures that it would take to identify and consult with "aboriginal people claiming an aboriginal interest in or to the area" (Tree Farm Licence No. 39, Haida Tree Farm Licence, para. 2.09(g)(ii)). However, the ultimate legal responsibility for consultation and accommodation rests with the Crown. The honour of the Crown cannot be delegated.[55]

That said, the duty to consult may have significant implications for third parties, which may, in turn, be of concern to governments from an economic development perspective. Whether consultation duties have been met in the context of third parties whose development would be of economic benefit in a particular place has been a subject of discussion at committee hearings in legislative bodies.[56] In *Hupacasath First Nation v. British Columbia (Minister of Forests)*, the British Columbia Supreme Court granted a judicial review of the Minister of Forest's decision to remove privately held lands from a particular tree farm license, where the government action had engaged the duty to consult.[57] The private landowners thus faced effects on their land use. In *Dene Tha' First Nation v. Canada (Minister of Environment)*, a failure to consult First Nations about the Mackenzie Gas Project led to an interim injunction against further steps on the project[58] — again affecting third parties and illustrating the importance for industry stakeholders of ensuring that governments carry out their duty to consult obligations.[59] Indeed, in situations where there has not been adequate consultation, protests and even blockades have emerged, with Indigenous communities claiming that particular developments have not complied with consultation requirements.[60] In Chapter 4 it is argued that, although the duty to consult does not apply to third parties in Canadian case law, an emerging practice of industry stakeholders and Aboriginal communities is nonetheless making corporate consultation with Aboriginal communities a non-optional practice.

The Crown would have the option of involving third parties — most likely the corporations involved in a project under consideration — in actually carrying out a consultation. Different industry stakeholders hold different views about this. Some were pleased by the decisions of some governments, like that of Saskatchewan, that consultation would be carried out solely by governments. Others indicated that they would like to have more of a role in consultations. What will work best on this front may depend on different circumstances and relationships in different provinces, as well as the nature of the matters on which Aboriginal communities are to be consulted. Much of how this proceeds will actually remain to be defined by the policies and practices of governments and Aboriginal communities.

One danger of having different industry stakeholders involved in carrying out consultations is that it may become difficult for an Aboriginal community to identify when it is or is not engaged in discussions that amount to consultation for purposes of the duty to consult. Various industry representatives may engage in discussions that might later be portrayed as part of a consultation process. This worry can be overcome by the government either carrying out all consultation itself or delegating its consultation roles quite explicitly where it does so. There will sometimes be advantages in delegating consultation. An industry stakeholder that is a proponent for a project will have a strong interest in seeing that consultation takes place efficiently and in accordance with the law. It may also have a very clear sense of the costs of different options for accommodation in a particular circumstance, and whether they will affect the viability of the project. The particular modalities of consultation delegated to third parties will be worked out not through further case law so much as through the policies and practices discussed in Chapter 4.

The constitutional duty to consult is one owed in a certain sense by an undivided Crown. The Crown can fail to meet its constitutional duties through problematic division of information within government as surely as through more deliberate failures to consult. If some departments are not well acquainted with consultation requirements, then they must seek advice from others. There must also be a sharing of information within government in respect of likely Aboriginal title, Aboriginal rights, and treaty rights claims.

The duty to consult is owed by the Crown to Aboriginal communities. Communities are the main rights-holders under s. 35. Analogously, the duty to consult is owed to communities rather than to individuals.[61] Once initiated, however, a duty to consult creates a set of shared responsibilities between the Crown and Aboriginal communities. If an Aboriginal community does not engage fully in a consultation process, for example, it may limit the Crown's duty to consult. In *Ahousaht Indian Band* v. *Canada (Minister of Fisheries & Oceans)*,[62] the First Nation's representative on an advisory committee did not attend early meetings of the committee. With the First Nation entering into the process late and later delaying matters by insisting on the adoption of a consultation protocol, the Crown did not breach the duty to consult when it went ahead with a pilot plan for commercial fishing without further bilateral discussions.[63] If an Aboriginal community indicates that it has acquiesced to a particular consultation procedure, this will also be a factor that may limit further consultation requirements on the part of the Crown.[64] Finally, if repeated requests for input from an Aboriginal community go unanswered, case law suggests this may terminate further requirements in the duty to consult on the issue on which those requests have been made.[65]

The responsibilities of the Aboriginal consultation partner will in some instances create real challenges for the community. In a small office, Aboriginal leaders may be expected to be simultaneously developing negotiation strategies on issues with the Crown, considering litigation on some issues, and now dealing with consultation issues. In some instances, consultation will involve significant quantities of paperwork, increasing as individuals seeking to avoid the risk of being accused of insufficient consultation add additional paperwork to what is sent out. Some of the panel members in the British Columbia Environmental Appeal Board May 2008 decision involving the Xats'ull First Nation's challenge to a mining discharge permit recently noted this effect. Panel member Derkaz wrote in her dissenting opinion:

[I]t is clear from the evidence of Mr. Michel and Mr. Phillips that the Xats'ull lack the financial and technical capacity to deal with the numerous referrals from companies seeking to carry on industrial activities that may affect their aboriginal interests. I have sympathy for the Xats'ull staff who are trying to deal with complicated applications without adequate resources. It is an unequal, and perhaps inherently unfair, relationship. This lack of capacity must be addressed if the province is going to live up to the vision expressed in the New Relationship with aboriginal people. However this is a matter beyond the jurisdiction of this Board.[66]

There will be times where it is appropriate that funding be made available to assist with consultation where the challenges are partly financial. Indeed, the Supreme Court of Canada's creation of the duty to consult has risked imposing on many Aboriginal communities quite costly activities that could have drawn on the same resource pool in use for longer-term negotiations and/or litigation. Many consultations will be technically complex, generating additional costs. The Métis Nation of Saskatchewan, to take one example, has estimated at $40,000 the costs it incurred in consulting with the Canadian Nuclear Safety Commission about abandoned uranium mines.[67] One First Nation contacted during the preparation of this book indicated that it was receiving in excess of a thousand consultation requests each year. In light of these challenges, several provinces, including Saskatchewan,[68] have moved to make funding available to facilitate consultation processes. However, merely making funding available is not necessarily a solution to some complex challenges. It is, in any case, clear that the capacity to engage in consultation processes flowing from the duty to consult is a real issue in the context of some Aboriginal communities' situations.

A further complication in some contexts will be the identification of the appropriate Aboriginal consultation partner(s). It is clear that the courts intend that consultation be carried out with communities and not typically with potentially affected individuals, but the identification of the appropriate representatives of a community is not always a simple matter.[69] One issue arises in the context of representation by a province-wide organization. For example, in *Native Council of Nova Scotia* v. *Canada (Attorney General)*, the Federal Court ended up rejecting the Native Council of Nova Scotia as an inappropriate consultation partner because it included some non-Mi'kmaq members, although it otherwise represented Nova Scotia Mi'kmaq on a province-wide basis.[70] The Federal Court of Appeal in the same case held, however, that it was not necessary to decide on the matter, as there was a lack of evidence to support the asserted right in any event.[71]

A complex set of issues arises in relation to consultation with Métis communities and individuals who identify as First Nations but are not recognized as such under the *Indian Act* — so-called "non-status Indians."[72] Surprisingly little case law has touched on the issue, although Thomas Isaac argues by inference from the cases in contexts involving First Nations, and the breadth of their language concerning "Aboriginal peoples," that a duty to consult Métis peoples is on solid legal ground even without Métis-specific case law.[73]

In *Labrador Métis Nation* v. *Newfoundland and Labrador*,[74] the Newfoundland Court of Appeal considered a situation where a number of disparate communities in Labrador had not self-identified as either Inuit or Métis but had claims to rights flowing from Aboriginal ancestry that would apply to either category of Aboriginality. The Court held that the Crown ought to have recognized a credible claim that led to a triggering of the duty to consult.[75] The Court was ready to accept the Labrador Métis Nation as an appropriate corporate agent to enforce the duty to consult through the lawsuit, seeing it as having been implicitly authorized by its members.[76] The Court also appears to have implicitly authorized that the form of consultation in the case could be appropriate notice to and opportunity to respond for the Labrador Métis Nation as a corporate body.[77] Thus, in some instances, Aboriginal communities without as much recognition in current governance structures will be able to constitute representative bodies that can fulfill their shared responsibilities in the consultation processes. This may represent an additional part of the solution to the capacity issues touched on above.

In its decision in *Re Imperial Oil Resources Ventures Ltd.*,[78] the Alberta Energy and Utilities Board applied conclusions from the *Labrador Métis Nation* litigation, while denying recognition to a number of groups asserting their claims to duties of consultation. The panel rejected the claims of two groups attempting to constitute themselves from individuals of already existing *Indian Act* bands, of an individual not connected to an Aboriginal community, and of an elders' society not showing itself to be the corporate agent of a rights-bearing Aboriginal community.[79]

Corporate and government stakeholders contacted during the preparation of this book tended to take the view that consultation with Métis communities would take place with Métis locals,[80] but there are complex and challenging questions on whether this is the preferable approach.[81] This topic will be subject to further discussion in Chapter 4, which examines briefly the policy frameworks enunciated by different Métis organizations. It bears noting for now that the rise of duty to consult issues has significant implications among Métis communities. Governments need to develop more effective policy in their relations to these communities. Because of the political power accruing to those acting as representatives in the context of consultations, it also falls to Métis communities to consider further the degree of formalization of their representative frameworks.

The challenges are perhaps more acute in the context of non-status Indians. The *Labrador Métis Nation* case opens the possibility of non-status communities being represented through appropriate representative organizations. The Congress of Aboriginal Peoples will presumably articulate a role for itself in this area, but the best representation of non-status communities on a particular issue may also be more localized. The duty to consult doctrine in some ways mandates a more formalized representative system as something that must be developed if Aboriginal communities are to benefit from consultation. If non-status communities do not formalize representative structures, they risk being further marginalized through the ongoing development of a doctrine that was intended to realize reconciliation with Aboriginal peoples.

This whole discussion on appropriate consultation partners raises additional issues. The government departments carrying out a consultation will need to assess carefully whether a particular body does or does not represent the relevant stakeholders. With the Native Council of Nova Scotia having been rejected but the Labrador Métis Nation having been recognized in cases that have entered into this area, the courts have not left things as clear as they could be. It is arguable, however, that the test implicit in the case law is whether the particular body either represents directly the interests of the relevant Aboriginal communities or is specifically authorized to do so, with an additional requirement in both cases being that it not be a representative body that represents potentially conflicting interests. This legal position creates some genuine practical challenges in implementation that will need to be worked through in the years ahead.

2.4 Judicial and Quasi-Judicial Intervention on the Duty to Consult

The constitutional duty to consult is an obligation intended to foster negotiation and nation-to-nation relationships over judicial dispute resolution
processes. However, the constitutional nature of the duty does mean that
it can be enforced through administrative tribunals or the courts if there
are concerns about the way in which consultations have (or have not) been
pursued in particular circumstances. This legal parameter can give rise to
some complex technical questions of jurisdiction that should not detain
us too long from the real question of when courts can become involved in
reviewing a particular duty to consult. Depending on the circumstances
and the rules governing the jurisdiction of the Federal Court, either the
provincial superior court system (the Court of Queen's Bench, in most
provinces) or the Federal Court system may have jurisdiction in a particular duty to consult case, to be determined on the basis of jurisdictional
rules beyond the scope of this book.[82] The two questions worthy of more
discussion here are to what degree courts will intervene or to what degree
they will defer to the choices of other decision-makers and what remedies
courts can use where they identify problems in a duty to consult process, as
well as how either of these differs (if at all) when a duty to consult matter
is before an administrative board or tribunal.

The courts have in a number of cases indicated that the matter under
examination in a challenge asserting a lack of fulfillment of the duty to
consult is the reasonableness of the government action in the circumstances.[83] The courts will not seek to intervene simply because there has
been some imperfection in the process; they are concerned with whether
there has been a reasonable effort at consultation and, where appropriate,
accommodation.[84] Have the Crown's actions been "within a range of reasonably defensible approaches"?[85] The standard in this area, according to
several courts touching on the matter, has not been altered by recent major developments in administrative law generally.[86] But if the Crown has
misconceived what is required of it, particularly by incorrectly concluding
that a duty to consult is at a lower end of the spectrum than it is, then this
may render its process unreasonable.[87] Thus, the courts show a meaningful
degree of deference to the development of reasonable processes and do not
seek to intervene in every instance, but they do stand ready to intervene
in an instance where the Crown party has fundamentally failed the duty
to consult.

For the government to establish that it has carried out consultation, it must be ready to provide a meaningful record to the courts. In a recent phase of the *Hupacasath First Nation* v. *British Columbia* case,[88] the British Columbia Supreme Court considered a 1663-page "consultation record" supplied by government lawyers. Much of it consisted of draft meeting notes rather than minutes and much of it contained specialized terminology not understandable to an outside reader; the Court concluded that the record did not "speak for itself."[89] To ensure that issues can be resolved effectively in the case of disputes arising over the process in a duty to consult, it is important for all stakeholders to keep detailed records of discussions and consultations that have taken place. Because it is a legal doctrine, the duty to consult entails a relatively formal process. Less formal discussions may be valuable in some contexts, but the degree of legal formality that informs the duty to consult obliges parties to think carefully about the effects of entering into informal discussions if there is any later dispute.

Once intervention in a duty to consult is under consideration, it is important to understand something of the possible remedies. First, before turning to remedies in relation to the duty to consult itself, in urgent circumstances a motion could be brought to restrain activities that would have an adverse effect on an Aboriginal community even prior to a judicial decision on the duty to consult.[90] If a court has concluded that there is a problem with the consultation process, the remedy depends in many respects on what stage matters have reached. In one sense, the appropriate remedy to insufficient consultation in a circumstance where consultation can still be ordered is to order that consultation.[91] This may be the case even where matters are some way along; in some circumstances it has been held appropriate to appoint a mediator if consultation is proving ineffective.[92]

Where decisions have already been made, the question may arise as to whether they should be stopped. As in other areas of law, the courts will typically not restrain dispositions of specific land where there is nothing unique about that land.[93] There will, though, be contexts where injunctions play a role. Various injunctions were used in the dispute between a junior exploration company and the Kitchenuhmaykoosib Inninuwug (KI), an Aboriginal people whose traditional territory was in the area under exploration. The corporation was under pressure to commence exploration to meet its obligations to its investors, particularly after the issuance of flow-through shares with deadlines for certain tax results, and gambled that the KI would not stop them. The Ontario Superior Court granted an injunction against the corporation, implying that it had brought the situation on itself. When an injunction was later granted against the Aboriginal community, some chose to defy it.[94]

There will be other contexts in which the remedy for a breach of the duty to consult that is a *fait accompli* is damages,[95] possibly at an elevated level that contains a punitive element against a government if its conduct has been particularly blameworthy.[96]

A court faced with the question of how to remedy a failure to meet the standards of the duty to consult obviously seeks to try to remedy the wrong, but should do so in a manner that is practical and fair to all who are affected by the remedy, including third-party stakeholders who played no role in the Crown's failure to meet its duties.[97] In some instances, the complex considerations at play may warrant a separate remedies hearing, at which it would presumably be possible to consider carefully the impact of different possible remedies on all stakeholders.[98] Some courts have indicated a reluctance to quash government decisions in instances where doing so may not be in the best interests of developments that may benefit everyone, including the Aboriginal communities involved.[99]

One could regard some dimensions of these remedial questions as, in some instances, actually being about the invocation of different bodies of law. This would appear to be one way of reading the central part of the recent decision of the Alberta Court of Queen's Bench in the *Tsuu T'ina Nation* case.[100] On this approach, one would look to whether a right had been proved or not and whether the government action at issue was complete. According to this approach, these contexts would invoke different bodies of law in terms of the application of the *Sparrow* justificatory standard in the context of completed action and proven rights and the *Haida Nation* approach in terms of anticipated action and unproven rights.[101] However, the significance of the duty to consult doctrine is that there can be a specific remedy for a violation of the duty to consult, as distinct from the remedy for the breach of an Aboriginal right, Aboriginal title, or a treaty right. It may be preferable not to think in terms of evoking these different bodies of law but in terms of the appropriate remedy on the duty to consult in different circumstances where it is easier or more difficult to undo certain decisions.

Courts' approaches to the remedial questions that arise when they are asked to intervene after a potential breach of the duty to consult show a degree of pragmatism and a recognition of a range of different considerations at play. They attempt to make the duty to consult meaningful without disrupting the expectations of innocent third parties, thus preferring a course that seeks to foster positive relationships among different stakeholders.

The recourse on a duty to consult matter may be in an administrative board or tribunal's jurisdiction before the matter ever goes before a court. Where such boards or tribunals have the power to decide questions of law, they are often described as quasi-judicial; and quasi-judicial administrative decision-making bodies, although not themselves courts, are like courts in that they are not themselves subject to the duty to consult Aboriginal communities.[102] However, recent appellate case law has made clear that quasi-judicial administrative boards and tribunals will review other government actors' efforts at consultation.[103] Indeed, there has been a specific rejection of some boards' previous "aversion to assessing the adequacy of consultation"[104] and an indication that such quasi-judicial bodies have "the obligation . . . to decide the constitutional question of whether the duty to consult exists and, if so, whether it has been discharged."[105] Many administrative boards and tribunals have in fact been making rulings on the acceptability or unacceptability of certain consultation processes.[106] It is also sometimes possible for such bodies to enter into supervision of fairly detailed terms they may impose on governments or other parties in relation to consultation as part of their regulatory approval processes.[107] These will be discussed further in Chapter 4, as administrative boards and tribunals have entered into fascinating policy-making roles in relation to the duty to consult. However, for the moment, we can say that the fundamental principles affecting their intervention on duty to consult issues should resemble the principles applied by the courts, subject to possible modification in the context of the greater specialization of boards and tribunals in those areas in which they may offer detailed assessment as well as meaningful ongoing supervision.

2.5 Conclusion

The lower courts developing the duty to consult case law pursuant to McLachlin C.J.C.'s guidance have been confronted with a number of pragmatic questions and have had to make a potentially theoretical and abstract doctrine work in the circumstances of real life. They have adopted some additional restraints on the triggering of the duty to avoid an impractical imposition of the duty to consult in an enormous range of circumstances. They have addressed some complex questions on the appropriate partners within a consultation, and they have sought to develop remedies in a manner that makes the duty to consult work effectively in the context of real-life considerations.

Making the duty to consult workable does not mean retreating from its aspirations; rather, it means fulfilling them and making them accessible. In the process, however, the highly generalized language of the Supreme Court of Canada has had to be attuned to real circumstances.

THREE

∞∞∞

THE DOCTRINAL SCOPE AND CONTENT
OF THE DUTY TO CONSULT

3.1 Introduction

The previous chapter set out the legal parameters of the duty to consult, including the contexts in which a duty to consult arises, who is engaged in the processes flowing from that duty, and approaches to remedies in relation to these processes. The next doctrinal question in terms of understanding the case law is the question of the scope and content of the duty to consult. The content of the duty in particular circumstances arises from a sort of spectrum analysis. As with any legal test that relies on multiple factors, there is a great deal of space for interpretation of the specific requirements in particular instances. This chapter, then, attempts to give the implications of this spectrum analysis more specific shape. Much of the law and writing on this spectrum analysis thus far, however, has said little on its implications for the crucial questions of accommodation and the possibility of the duty to consult implying certain sorts of compensation, so the chapter then turns to examine those issues.

A key aim in this chapter is to say something about the nature of a "good consultation," although one must be mindful from the outset that a good consultation ought not to be limited to the elements prescribed by legal doctrine. Good consultations are about developing relationships and finding ways of living together in the encounter that history has thrust upon us. Focusing too narrowly on the legal form of the duty may contain hidden dangers to deeper forms of consultation and reconciliation. Focusing on the legal doctrine may result in a legalistic approach to relationships that entails extensive attempts to formalize and document discussions, which might well not be what best contributes to a relationship of trust. Later in this chapter, we will return to attempting to characterize a good consultation, with part of the suggestion being the importance of going beyond the elements prescribed by legal doctrine.

3.2 Content of the Duty to Consult

The triggering of a duty to consult in particular circumstances opens the further question of the scope of the duty in those circumstances, as it can range from a fairly minimal notice requirements to a thorough duty to consult Aboriginal communities and accommodate their interests. Throughout the spectrum, each situation requires a meaningful effort by the government to act in a manner consistent with the honour of the Crown.[1] This means that the government must act adequately for the circumstances in providing notice of an issue and appropriate timelines for response, disclosing relevant information, engaging in meaningful discussion, responding to concerns raised in those discussions, and, in appropriate circumstances, accommodating Aboriginal interests.[2]

The principle that the government must act consistently with the honour of the Crown co-exists with a recognition of the principle that "the process itself would likely fall to be examined on a standard of reasonableness. Perfect satisfaction is not required."[3] The Federal Court of Appeal thus ruled in June 2008 in *Ahousaht Indian Band* v. *Canada (Minister of Fisheries & Oceans)* that "reasonable efforts to inform and consult ... would normally suffice to discharge the duty."[4] This latter principle, however, does not mean that governments should be guided by anything less than honour. The content of the duty to consult is informed by honour, but review of consultation efforts in particular circumstances is limited to review for reasonable content.

3.2(a) Introducing the Spectrum of Requirements on the Duty to Consult

The Supreme Court of Canada's case law provides the initial guidance on the spectrum of requirements within the duty to consult. In general terms, McLachlin C.J.C. explains in *Haida Nation*:

> The content of the duty to consult and accommodate varies with the circumstances. Precisely what duties arise in different situations will be defined as the case law in this emerging area develops. In general terms, however, it may be asserted that the scope of the duty is proportionate to a preliminary assessment of the strength of the case supporting the existence of the right or title, and to the seriousness of the potentially adverse effect upon the right or title claimed.[5]

This spectrum analysis, of course, differs in a significant manner in the treaty rights context as compared to the Aboriginal title or Aboriginal rights context. In the former, the existence of a particular right will typically already be clear, and appropriate consultation hinges pivotally on the seriousness of the potential impact on the treaty right. This is the point the Supreme Court of Canada makes clear in the *Mikisew Cree* case:

> In the case of a treaty the Crown, as a party, will always have notice of its contents. The question in each case will therefore be to determine the degree to which conduct contemplated by the Crown would adversely affect those rights so as to trigger the duty to consult. *Haida Nation* and *Taku River* set a low threshold. The flexibility lies not in the trigger ("might adversely affect it") but in the variable content of the duty once triggered.[6]

In any event, there is a need for further clarification of the requirement of "meaningful consultation appropriate to the circumstances."[7] The Court suggests that the content of this requirement can be described appropriately in terms of a spectrum of requirements. Chief Justice McLachlin provides the Court's initial outline:

> At one end of the spectrum lie cases where the claim to title is weak, the Aboriginal right limited, or the potential for infringement minor. In such cases, the only duty on the Crown may be to give notice, disclose information, and discuss any issues raised in response to the notice. . . . At the other end of the spectrum lie cases where a strong *prima facie* case for the claim is established, the right and potential

infringement is of high significance to the Aboriginal peoples, and the risk of non-compensable damage is high. In such cases deep consultation, aimed at finding a satisfactory interim solution, may be required. While precise requirements will vary with the circumstances, the consultation required at this stage may entail the opportunity to make submissions for consideration, formal participation in the decision-making process, and provision of written reasons to show that Aboriginal concerns were considered and to reveal the impact they had on the decision. This list is neither exhaustive, nor mandatory for every case. The government may wish to adopt dispute resolution procedures like mediation or administrative regimes with impartial decision-makers in complex or difficult cases. . . . Between these two extremes of the spectrum just described, will lie other situations. Every case must be approached individually. Each must also be approached flexibly, since the level of consultation required may change as the process goes on and new information comes to light. The controlling question in all situations is what is required to maintain the honour of the Crown and to effect reconciliation between the Crown and the Aboriginal peoples with respect to the interests at stake.[8]

In the *Haida Nation* case itself, there was a strong *prima facie* claim to Aboriginal title, and the contemplated granting of tree farm licenses affected forests in a manner having potentially serious impacts on the Haida Nation, so the Court indicated that the duty to consult in the circumstances would be above the minimal level and, indeed, would likely extend to a degree of accommodation.[9] Where there had been no consultation at all, the Crown had fallen short of its duty to consult.

In the companion judgment in the *Taku River Tlingit First Nation* case,[10] the acceptance of the community's claim into treaty negotiations demonstrated the relative strength of its *prima facie* claims, and the potential effect on the community of proposed road construction was significant, so the Court again indicated that the content of the duty to consult in the circumstances would extend beyond the minimal requirements of notice, disclosure, and consultation to include what it termed a "level of responsiveness to [the community's] concerns."[11] In this case, however, the Court held that a process of consultations under the provincial *Environmental Assessment Act* had been sufficient to meet the requirements of the duty to consult as it offered meaningful opportunities for consultation and was leading toward accommodations within appropriate stages of the development of the project under consideration.[12]

In this latter case, the duty to consult with Aboriginal communities was fulfilled in the context of environmental assessment procedures; however, it was in the specific terms of an Aboriginal consultation process within the broader environmental assessment.[13] Some stakeholders in the resource industries have concerns about the potential consequences of Aboriginal law duty to consult practices becoming separate from other consultation processes; they are concerned that a consultation process that excludes other stakeholders may not meet the requirements of administrative law natural justice for others.[14]

At the same time, others have concerns with trying to fit Aboriginal consultation too directly into other processes.[15] It is clear that the law will not inherently treat a simple public notice under an environmental consultation process as fulfilling requirements within the duty to consult Aboriginal communities[16] — although this conclusion depends on the position of particular circumstances on the spectrum analysis. In the specific circumstances of development on private land near a reserve, for instance, the requirements of the duty to consult may not include an enhanced right of notice but instead be met by the standard process of advertising and sending notice of a hearing on the matter.[17] The relationship of appropriate consultation with Aboriginal communities to other consultation processes mandated by administrative law principles or specific environmental assessment regimes will thus depend on specific circumstances.

The spectrum on the duty to consult thus arises from two principal factors: the strength of the Aboriginal claim, and the seriousness of the impact of contemplated government action on the interests underlying that claim. These two elements of the spectrum analysis track roughly the two elements within the triggering test: knowledge of the Aboriginal claim, and the possibility of contemplated government action having an adverse impact on underlying Aboriginal interests.[18] Where these preconditions do not attain the relevant threshold levels discussed above, there is no content to the duty to consult and, indeed, no duty to consult.[19] At the other extreme, in circumstances with a strong Aboriginal claim and serious potential impacts on it, there would be a duty to consult the Aboriginal community and accommodate relevant Aboriginal interests.

The first element in the spectrum test, the *prima facie* strength of the claim for Aboriginal title, an Aboriginal right, or a treaty right actually falls to be determined to a degree based on jurisprudence from other areas of Aboriginal law and the evidence that fits those requirements. It is jurisprudence on Aboriginal title claims, Aboriginal rights claims, and treaty rights claims that speaks to the strength of the relevant claims for a duty to consult and evidence of those underlying claims that affects the *prima facie* strength element.

Frequently, all the relevant evidence is not immediately available to those assessing the *prima facie* strength of the Aboriginal claim. A government department considering the content of the duty to consult in particular circumstances may need to seek information from other departments with more specific knowledge of the particular claim. Even then, however, governments may well be operating without knowledge of all the specific evidence that an Aboriginal community may be able to present, such as the content of elders' testimony that may not be known to others. Nonetheless, a rough estimate of the *prima facie* strength of the claim may well flow reasonably from a preliminary assessment of known evidence concerning the connection of the claim to traditional territories and practices, from a comparison of the claim to other kinds of claims that have been successful or unsuccessful, and from a basic estimation of the likely success of a particular kind of claim.

Several issues are worthy of discussion in terms of their relationship to this dimension of the spectrum analysis. First, there is an element of shared responsibility over the identification of the rights claim and its assessment. On the one hand, the Crown has an obligation to attempt to identify the relevant rights claims; in a case where the federal Department of Transport did not conceive a claim correctly, the courts were ready to conclude that this made its resulting process of consultation unreasonable.[20] On the other hand, once notified of government action, Aboriginal communities have a responsibility to identify rights claims potentially affected; failure to do so may preclude further consultation requirements.[21] Thus, the Crown has a responsibility to identify accurately whether a duty to consult is triggered; thereafter, there is a shared responsibility through the initial phases of consultation to identify what is at stake so that appropriate further consultation or accommodation can be implemented.

An awkward situation may arise when more than one Aboriginal community has made a claim to title or a right that cannot be shared. The British Columbia Environmental Appeal Board dealt with such a situation in a recent decision involving the Xats'ull First Nation appealing a permit issued for the discharge of contaminants from a mining operation on the basis of an alleged failure to consult,[22] and the Environmental Appeal Board suggested that the Aboriginal title claim of the Xats'ull was weaker in parts of the claimed territory where their claim overlapped with those of other First Nations.[23] This was particularly problematic for the Xats'ull, as the areas closest to the discharge point and thus most likely to be affected by it were the areas where their title claim was now weakest.[24] The presence of overlapping claims has also been argued as a factor in the context of other duty to consult litigation.[25] Where there are overlapping claims, it would appear to weaken the probability of each Aboriginal community being successful in its claim, and it thus becomes something, according to the doctrine, that lessens the content of the duty to consult *vis-à-vis* each potentially affected Aboriginal community. This factor within the duty to consult analysis may be one additional reason for Aboriginal communities to seek to come to agreement on the extent of their respective claims.

A third complicated situation is where there has been a past surrender of a particular Aboriginal right or of Aboriginal title. Such an issue went before the Ontario courts in *Hiawatha First Nation* v. *Ontario (Minister of Environment)*.[26] Seven First Nations claimed that the Ontario government had failed to consult with them in the context of negotiations with private land developers on land that encompassed burial sites. The Court held, however, that there had been a surrender of Aboriginal claims over the lands in a 1923 treaty, and, as a result, the Crown owed no duty of consultation. Some commentators have cited this case as implying fairly definitively that there will be no duty to consult in the context of rights that have been surrendered.[27]

This conclusion, however, is rendered less clear by the Yukon Court of Appeal in its August 2008 decision in *Little Salmon/Carmacks First Nation* v. *Yukon (Minister of Energy, Mines, and Resources)*.[28] In this case, the terms of a modern treaty explicitly excluded requirements for consultation other than in specific contexts and circumstances, but the Yukon Court of Appeal nonetheless considered that there were further consultation requirements. If this conclusion stands on appeal, it would carry the implication that even surrender provisions in treaties may not definitively remove related requirements in the duty to consult. The matter may come to be tested in other contexts. For instance, in the *Platinex Inc.* v. *Kitchenuhmaykoosib Inninuwug First Nation* litigation, the treaty arrangements in place foresaw that the Crown might take up land for mining and that this might affect

Aboriginal harvesting rights, but there was still considered to be a duty to consult the Aboriginal community when this took place, which the Crown had met through the establishment of a memorandum of understanding with the mining company involved. The case has gone through several injunction stages, with significant controversy ensuing.[29] The effects of surrender provisions are going to depend on a variety of circumstances in a particular context, and all should be on notice that surrender provisions, although on some case law potentially removing a duty to consult, must be analyzed with exacting care in each instance.

The second element in the spectrum test is the seriousness of the impact of contemplated government action on the affected Aboriginal community. This has not attracted as much case law on complicating elements, but it would be fair to say that an important factor will be whether government action has potentially irreversible effects as opposed to more transitory ones.[30] In the case of potentially irreversible effects on vital Aboriginal interests, the expected degree of consultation — and quite possibly accommodation — will be high.[31] Furthermore, the kind of Aboriginal interest at stake may affect the assessment of the seriousness of the impact: a government impact on an economic interest will possibly attract a lesser consultation requirement within the spectrum than a government impact on certain kinds of cultural interests.

3.2(b) Specific Factors within the Consultation Requirements

Chief Justice McLachlin attempts to speak to what the content of the duty to consult will be in particular circumstances, offering a broad spectrum analysis; within this spectrum, the duty may range from one "to give notice, disclose information, and discuss any issues raised in response to the notice" through to instances where "deep consultation, aimed at finding a satisfactory interim solution, may be required" and "the consultation required at this stage may entail the opportunity to make submissions for consideration, formal participation in the decision-making process, and provision of written reasons to show that Aboriginal concerns were considered and to reveal the impact they had on the decision."[32]

Varying possibilities thus emerge for the content of the duty to consult in particular circumstances. It may range from minimal notice, disclosure, and responsiveness through to deep consultation that follows more complex administrative law approaches, seeks to develop interim solutions, and potentially makes use of appropriate dispute resolution procedures. On the one hand, the Supreme Court of Canada case law describes the application of these different requirements in terms of the application of the factors of the spectrum analysis. On the other, it roots them in the more principled but also more general analysis of what will best maintain the honour of the Crown and further the ends of reconciliation. As discussed in Chapter 1, these latter principles may not actually point in a single direction but in various directions. The determination of the content of the duty to consult in particular circumstances remains as much art as science.

Nonetheless, the goal of consultation in each instance is an engagement by the Crown with Aboriginal communities in the manner necessary to make the duty to consult a meaningful enactment of its underlying goals. This can be seen through various factors in the consultation requirements, including the time for consultation, the expectations of the notice to the Aboriginal consultation partner, the opportunities offered for responses from the Aboriginal consultation partner, and the duty of accommodation where appropriate. Analyzing each element in terms of what makes the consultation meaningful helps to define the content of that element.

For example, the duty to consult in particular circumstances may well apply over a significant period of time and not be fulfilled through a one-off consultation. What determines this is what is necessary to the appropriate consultation requirements given where one is on the spectrum. Where it is important to the meaningfulness of the expected level of consultation, it may be essential for the Aboriginal consultation partner(s) to be engaged from the beginning and/or involved through to the end. An example of the former arises in the *Dene Tha'* case, in which the Federal Court held that the meaningfulness of consultation was undermined by the fact that the Dene Tha' had not been engaged in consultation from the beginning of planning on a pipeline that was to pass through their traditional territory.[33] An example of the latter arises in *Ka'a'gee Tu First Nation* v. *Canada (Indian Affairs and Northern Development)*[34] in which the Federal Court held that there had been a breach of the constitutional duty to consult because, although the Ka'a'gee Tu had had the chance to participate in some consultations, there was a final stage of decision-making with different elements under consideration in which they had no opportunity to be consulted. What is at issue in each case is when involvement in consultation is meaningful, and the courts have repeatedly drawn on this concept of what timeline makes consultation "meaningful."[35]

Obviously, the timeline of when consultation must begin relates back to the triggering questions discussed in the previous chapter. There is a danger in looking at a course of government action in retrospect, in that one can come to the view that consultation should have been present from the beginning based on later consequences that were not identified at the first moment, such as where government awareness was reasonably limited or where the government's contemplated action evolved over the course of the project. This imposes an impossible standard on governments. That being said, there is also a danger in not identifying the full scope of what is under contemplation. The duty to consult test calls for careful analysis in light of its purposes.

In terms of notice to an Aboriginal consultation partner, it is clear that an overly short comment period may undermine the effect of a notice, and that a notice must be directed specifically to an Aboriginal community — as opposed to, as in one case, simply being posted on the Internet for whoever happens to come across it.[36] Again, what is important is that which will further meaningful consultation — meaningful in terms of responding to the goals of entering into the consultation process in the first place. Thinking of the content of the duty to consult in these terms, of course, makes crucial how we understand the duty to consult in theoretical terms, such as in the models raised in Chapter 1. What makes consultation meaningful under one model may differ under another.

This chapter turns to the scope of accommodation in appropriate circumstances, but, for the moment, we can conclude that the fundamental parameters on a consultation call, at a minimum, for appropriate timing, appropriate notice, and a meaningful opportunity to respond.

3.2(c) The Consultation Spectrum

Just how extensive each of the requirements is in particular circumstances falls to be determined on the spectrum, based on the *prima facie* strength of the Aboriginal claim and the potential impact of the Crown action. Some governmental policies, building on the case law, have sought to express the spectrum and its implications in terms of a matrix of levels of consultation.

The Saskatchewan government's draft consultation policy includes the following matrix:

Project or Government Action	First Nation and Métis Rights in Traditional Territories				
	No Demonstrated Impact	Low Impact on Rights	Occasional Impact on Rights	Moderate Impact on Rights	Intensive Impact on Rights and/or Culturally Significant Site/s
Major Project or Government Action	Notification	Moderate Consultation	Intensive Consultation	Intensive Consultation	Intensive Consultation
Moderate to Large Project or Government Action	Notification	Limited Consultation	Moderate Consultation	Intensive Consultation	Intensive Consultation
Minor Project or Government Action	No Notification	Notification	Limited Consultation	Moderate Consultation	Moderate Consultation

Table: Matrix on Consultation Intensity[37]

This sort of graphic representation is potentially helpful in understanding how to determine a level of consultation from the combined dimensions of the *prima facie* strength of an Aboriginal claim and the scale of potential impact on Aboriginal interests. Note, however, that the Saskatchewan matrix does not use those factors as the axes, opting instead for the impact on the Aboriginal right and the scope of the project having these impacts.[38] These factors seek to interpret pragmatically the requirements on governments, scaling the depth of the consultation to the scale of the project and thus ensuring that consultation is economically manageable in the context of different projects. This matrix is lacking a foundation in the doctrinal case law. Consultation in Saskatchewan operates in a different context than it does in British Columbia. A Saskatchewan consultation will frequently pertain to treaty rights rather than any other Aboriginal right, and Aboriginal title claims have a very limited application, if any, in the Saskatchewan context. (There are outstanding issues about whether the Dakota Sioux, who did not have a treaty relationship because they were an American Aboriginal community that moved to Canada, might have any kind of Aboriginal title claim.) The result is that the *prima facie* strength of an Aboriginal claim will typically not be a distinguishing factor in different circumstances — although the strength of different treaty interpretations sometimes will be — leaving the seriousness of impact on the relevant Aboriginal interests the key distinguishing factor set out in the case law.[39] If even a minor project will have an intensive, deep impact on Aboriginal interests, there is no particular justification for treating it as giving rise to only "moderate" consultation. This matrix thus introduces a factor not authorized by the case law to date.

Nonetheless, thinking of the spectrum in terms of a matrix is helpful in considering the congruent effects of the two major factors: the *prima facie* strength of the claim and the scale of potential impact on the Aboriginal or treaty right. The doctrine has allowed for an interplay between these elements, with the deepest consultation required when there is both a strong *prima facie* claim and a major potential impact, a much more limited consultation when there is a weak *prima facie* claim and little potential impact, and a moderate level of consultation in the intermediate cases.

3.2(d) An Example: The Keystone Pipeline Case

An example of how a court approaches matters may help clarify the content of the duty to consult. The May 2009 judgment of the Federal Court in *Brokenhead Ojibway Nation v. Canada (Attorney General)*[40] is a recent example of a case that has been closely watched as testing the implications of the duty to consult in the context of a set of pipeline projects, one of which was the Keystone Pipeline, by which name the case has become known by many. Just what approach the courts take to the duty to consult in this case is thought to have significant implications for other resource development projects, notably the proposed MacKenzie Valley Pipeline, although other situations will obviously fall ultimately to be tested on their own facts and processes.

The seven First Nations seeking declaratory relief against the pipelines running through their traditional lands in southern Manitoba asserted that there had been inadequate consultation. Officials to whom they had written had not engaged with them. The Prime Minister, the Minister of Indian Affairs, other ministers, and the Secretary of the Governor in Council (GIC) had not even acknowledged their correspondence.[41] Their concerns related both to the site-specific impacts of the projects, many of which were considered in National Energy Board proceedings, and broader concerns about the impact of the pipelines on future treaty land claims or the spiritual relation of First Nations to their traditional territories. The Attorney General of Canada argued that consultation had taken place through the engagement of corporate entities with the First Nations and the National Energy Board — in effect, holding that the Board's conduct of its role helped fulfill the duty to consult. Significantly, Barnes J. in the Federal Court judgment of May 2009 holds that the use of existing regulatory processes may satisfy the duty to consult, depending on the overriding responsibility of the Crown to ensure the adequacy of these processes in the circumstances at issue.[42] This latter point is significant, for it implies that there could effectively be, in some contexts, an obligation to enhance regulatory processes, at least if they are meant to be relied upon as playing a part in consultation.

In the judgment, Barnes J. emphasizes "the principle that the content of the duty to consult with First Nations is proportionate to both the potential strength of the claim or right asserted and the anticipated impact of a development or project on these asserted interests."[43] This invocation of the spectrum analysis situates the case within the overall legal framework of the content of the duty to consult. Evidence of extensive engagement around site-specific concerns and the National Energy Board's ability to scrutinize those site-specific arrangements went far in convincing Barnes J. that there had been appropriate consultation in some respects.[44] Possible concerns remained if there were more overarching rights threatened. However, Barnes J. emphasized that "[t]here must be some unresolved non-negligible impact arising from such a development to engage the Crown's duty to consult."[45] This statement may appear to refer to the triggering of the duty, but the point, rather, is that there may be a stronger duty to consult in relation to site-specific impacts and less or no duty to consult on broader matters where there is not a sufficiently strong impact demonstrated on other rights. The content of the duty to consult can vary even within the context of a single project or issue, with stronger content to the duty in some respects than in others. In this case, Barnes J. seeks to distinguish the demonstrated impact from that in other cases[46] and notes that the pipeline projects are largely on private land — land that had been previously developed and was not readily susceptible of treaty rights claims in any event.[47]

What is interesting here is not so much the conclusion — the case is potentially still subject to appeal — as the analysis. It is based on a careful application of the spectrum analysis within a specific factual context; this analysis can involve comparisons to other cases and even the drawing of distinctions between different potential forms of consultation in the case at hand. When Barnes J. concludes that any duty to consult was met by the proceedings of the National Energy Board and the opportunities it offered for consultation and accommodation, the decision is geared to analyzing how potential impacts on Aboriginal and treaty rights needed to be considered in light of the impacts at issue. The content of the duty to consult in any given case will be contextual and fact-specific, albeit within the broad framework this chapter has outlined in terms of the spectrum analysis and the fundamental components of consultation: notice and appropriate timelines for response, appropriate disclosure of relevant information, meaningful discussion appropriate to the circumstances, responding to concerns raised in discussions, and potentially accommodating concerns in appropriate circumstances. It is to some of the broader questions around accommodation that we now turn.

3.3 The Duty to Accommodate

The Supreme Court of Canada's decision in *Haida Nation* makes clear that accommodation will not always be required in the context of consultation, but indicates that it will sometimes be required as a component of the duty to consult. Chief Justice McLachlin describes these principles:

> [T]he effect of good faith consultation may be to reveal a duty to accommodate. Where a strong *prima facie* case exists for the claim, and the consequences of the government's proposed decision may adversely affect it in a significant way, addressing the Aboriginal concerns may require taking steps to avoid irreparable harm or to minimize the effects of infringement, pending final resolution of the underlying claim.[48]

Any such accommodation will be developed in the context of complex competing interests, with McLachlin C.J.C. going on to write:

> Balance and compromise are inherent in the notion of reconciliation. Where accommodation is required in making decisions that may adversely affect as yet unproven Aboriginal rights and title claims, the Crown must balance Aboriginal concerns reasonably with the potential impact of the decision on the asserted right or title and with other societal interests.[49]

The language here is quite open-textured, and other cases have done little to define further the requirements of accommodation. Industry stakeholders contacted during the writing of this book identified uncertainty about the legal requirements in terms of accommodation as one of the most vexing dimensions of the duty to consult doctrine. To this point, accommodation is described in the case law simply in terms of what interim arrangements will avoid irreparable effects on Aboriginal interests and what interim arrangements will minimize harm to Aboriginal interests, all in the context of the underlying aims of the duty to consult doctrine.[50] This latter point is an important one. In the *Dene Tha'* case, for instance, Phelan J. emphasized that consultation should be geared to reconciliation and, indeed, suggested that the "goal of consultation is not to be narrowly interpreted as the mitigation of adverse effects on Aboriginal rights and/or title."[51] This nuance provides an example of where the different theoretical perspectives one could take to the duty to consult have different implications for a fundamental matter like the accommodations implied.

These principles admittedly leave much undecided to this point, and there is much room for the case law to develop in this area. Interestingly, to date, the cases that have ended up in litigation have tended to be more about whether there was a recognition of the need for consultation or an adequate effort at consultation rather than whether there was an appropriate accommodation of interests identified through well-functioning consultations. This may mean that governments have made good faith efforts when Aboriginal interests were identified, thus avoiding litigation, or it may simply mean that the duty to consult remains in its early days.

Any accommodations arising from consultations are going to be fact-specific. They ought to be oriented to the principles behind the duty to consult and advance these principles as best as possible. The debates around these principles need not postpone practical action. Where one routing of a proposed road has a significant impact on an Aboriginal community's interests, and it is reasonably possible to reroute the road, doing so will both minimize the impact on the Aboriginal community and further the reconciliation of diverse communities in the Canadian federation. Some accommodations will simply amount to practical adjustments to plans such that they are taking account of Aboriginal interests in a reasonable manner. The tougher questions arise in circumstances where the necessary adjustments would come at a high cost, particularly those that would make a project no longer viable. In those circumstances, there must be a weighing of the different interests with an openness to talking them through. No doctrine can make for easy choices.

3.4 The Duty to Consult and Economic Accommodation

One particularly uncertain element of accommodation relates to so-called "economic accommodation." Where judges have engaged directly with duty to consult situations that potentially raise "economic accommodation" as one of the matters at issue, they have been circumspect. The implications of any decision, obviously, are significant because of the possible precedent for other situations. Justice Neilson acknowledged as much in her decision in the *Wii'litswx* case:

> Turning to Gitanyow's interest in revenue sharing, the economic component of aboriginal interests is clearly a significant issue, with wide-ranging repercussions for all citizens of British Columbia. In my view, in the course of balancing Gitanyow's interests against other societal interests, the Crown may be justifiably wary of dealing with revenue sharing on an individualized basis. For example, I do not find it unreasonable for the Crown to decline to consider Gitanyow's claim for substantial sums as its share of past and future logging revenue until the ramifications of such an approach can be considered at a broader level. I am satisfied that, in the interim, the periodic payments made by the Crown to support ongoing initiatives, and the development of a consultation framework to consider alternative means of accommodating the economic aspects of aboriginal interests, suggest good faith, ongoing consultation and accommodation on the part of the Crown to advance this process. It is regrettable that this initiative appears to be moving at such a slow pace, but at present it apparently has the blessing of both the Crown and the First Nations Forest Council.[52]

The language of "economic accommodation" is arguably preferable to that of "compensation," which is used in some other contexts. The concept of economic accommodation is broader than that of compensation, and it allows for a more nuanced consideration of possible win-win combinations that build economic activity within Aboriginal communities. That being said, some of the case law refers to the possibility of compensation for a breach of the duty to consult once that breach is a *fait accompli* and reversing a course of action to enforce the duty to consult is no longer viable.[53] In certain limited circumstances, compensation may become the relevant form of economic accommodation.

A claim that has been put before the courts by the Beaver Lake Cree Nation pushes compensation questions in the direction of retroactive claims for lack of consultation in the past.[54] The Beaver Lake Cree seek compensation for non-consultation in relation to over 16,000 permits granted for oil and gas activities on its traditional lands, stretching back to the mid-1990s. What will become of this action remains to be seen. The decisions of courts in such cases may have major implications for the duty to consult, and, indeed, for relations between Aboriginal and non-Aboriginal Canadians for years to come.

Acknowledging that there are many uncertainties remaining, it is nonetheless possible to comment on differing possibilities for economic accommodation in different places. British Columbia's lack of historical treaties means that much of the province is subject to Aboriginal title claims. Effects on Aboriginal title will almost invariably give rise to claims for economic accommodation because Aboriginal title is an interest in land which, while *sui generis*, is more analogous to fee simple than other interests arising from Aboriginal rights[55] and has what the courts have sometimes called an "inescapable economic component."[56] Where the scope of the duty to consult concerns consultation around the content of treaty rights, such as in Saskatchewan, the role of economic accommodation is not as clear. Aboriginal communities have certainly asserted that their understanding of the spirit of the treaties would give rise to a role for economic accommodation and resource revenue-sharing.[57] Governments have a different perspective on this.

Ongoing discussions around economic accommodation will shape significantly what the duty to consult means in pragmatic terms. Revenue-sharing may be appropriate in some circumstances, particularly where Aboriginal communities hold a right that has economic dimensions, such as Aboriginal title. Even in circumstances where it is not legally required, governments will no doubt consider the possibility, not least because of potential inequalities arising between different Aboriginal communities if some are excluded from economic accommodation because of the happenstance of history. However, economic accommodation may take place in ways other than revenue-sharing, and these may include other impact benefit arrangements that further the interests of various parties. What will be necessary is to continue working toward relationships of trust that give rise to reasonable arrangements that can be accepted on all sides. As aptly put by Southin J.A. of the British Columbia Court of Appeal,

[t]he core of accommodation is the balancing of interests and the reaching of a compromise until such time as claimed rights to property are finally resolved. In relatively undeveloped areas of the province, I should think accommodation might take a multiplicity of forms such as a sharing of mineral or timber resources. One could also envisage employment agreements or land transfers and the like. This is a developing area of the law and it is too early to be at all categorical about the ambit of appropriate accommodative solutions that have to work not only for First Nations people but for all of the populace having a broad regard to the public interest.[58]

3.5 Legally Acceptable Consultation and Good Consultation

A legally acceptable consultation, as discussed in the previous two chapters, must be initiated at an appropriate stage, such that there is meaningful discussion about a particular strategy or plan. There must be an identification of the Aboriginal communities potentially affected and an identification of contact people in those communities. There must be appropriate forms of notice given and further information made available where necessary for meaningful consultation. In cases of deeper consultation, it will be necessary to convene meetings to discuss the concerns that are arising. In any case, it is necessary to have lines of communication genuinely open to hear the implications of Aboriginal interests. In cases where accommodation issues arise, it is necessary to seek appropriate accommodations of Aboriginal interests in light of the issues expressed in consultations.

Establishing legal norms for the purposes of reconciliation may be necessary to promote efforts at reconciliation and to protect the rights of different parties, but if this encourages parties on either side to seek to do the minimum permitted under the legal norms, it will not have the positive outcomes that real efforts at consultation and reconciliation could have. Some have raised the concern that governments may exploit the fact that the duty to consult does not include a veto by Aboriginal communities to authorize developments after an attempt at consultation, imposing their views in the shorter term but with a risk of longer-term problems.[59] Consultation has much more potential than this scenario. Consultation embodies the possibility of genuinely hearing one another and seeking reconciliations that work in the shorter-term while opening the door for negotiations of longer-term solutions to unsolved legal problems. Those potentially engaged with consultations, whether governments, Aboriginal communities, or corporate stakeholders, ought to bear in mind not only their doctrinal legal position but the longer-term prospects for trust and reconciliation that will enable all to live together in the years ahead.

ooooo

THE LAW IN ACTION
OF THE DUTY TO CONSULT

4.1 Introduction: The Concept of the Law in Action

It is customary in a legal text to write as if the basic legislation and case law on an issue sum up all there is to know on the law. Roscoe Pound famously resisted this approach, offering in 1910 a call for an analysis of not just the "law in books" but the "law in action."[1] Pound argued that the two would diverge, particularly in circumstances where social change rendered the settled law less relevant, where rigid legislation did not allow flexibility, and where administrative machinery was not fully functioning.[2] The basic concept of the "law in action" is more inspired than the analysis Pound develops, for there are other reasons why the "law in action" might differ from the "law in books," some of them originating from reasons opposite to the ones Pound cites. For example, there will be circumstances in which high-level appellate court pronouncements will provide insufficient detail for doctrine to work in applied contexts. Nonetheless, Pound's basic concept resonates in powerful ways, calling for attention beyond the law books to the law in action.

Pound's basic impulse to urge attention to the law in action does not strike readers today as shocking. Indeed, 100 years later there is danger that "legal realism" may undermine the careful analysis of doctrine and legal reasoning that is vital to the legal academy in helping to maintain the rule of law. But the duty to consult is one area in which one would end up with a rather limited view of the law without some attempt to come to grips with the law in action of the duty to consult. The duty to consult is being shaped not just in the courts but in the day-to-day policies and practices of governments, Aboriginal communities, and industry stakeholders. In the end, as will be argued later in this chapter, the coalescence of their efforts at implementing the law into action may well describe something vitally important about the law in this area.

4.2 Development of Governmental Consultation Policies

Provincial governmental policies related to the duty to consult have already been recognized as having significance for the doctrine. Note, for instance, the Supreme Court of Canada's reference in *Haida Nation* to the possible value of provincial policy:

> It should be observed that, since October 2002, British Columbia has had a Provincial Policy for Consultation with First Nations to direct the terms of provincial ministries' and agencies' operational guidelines. Such a policy, while falling short of a regulatory scheme, may guard against unstructured discretion and provide a guide for decision-makers.[3]

Provincial governments have taken important steps in recent years toward developing duty to consult policies, with a number of provinces having adopted such policies, on an interim basis in a number of cases, but at least moving toward more finalized policies. Formal provincial consultation policies that are publicly available have been developed or are under development in Alberta,[4] British Columbia,[5] Saskatchewan,[6] Manitoba,[7] Ontario,[8] Quebec,[9] and Nova Scotia.[10] The federal government has also moved to develop a consultation policy.[11]

The process of developing the policy framework in Saskatchewan illustrates certain challenges in relation to the stability of policy frameworks on the duty to consult. The government issued duty to consult guidelines to relevant stakeholders in June 2006. These guidelines, however, were based simply on legal doctrine as assessed by government lawyers without consultation with Aboriginal leaders, which led to criticism both from the Aboriginal community and the opposition Saskatchewan Party at the time.[12] Following the fall 2007 election the new government launched a process on the duty to consult policy, releasing an interim policy in January 2008 before holding consultations with stakeholders that culminated in a Roundtable in Saskatoon in May 2008.[13] This led to a draft document issued in December 2008,[14] which again drew criticism, but the government hoped to move toward a final document nonetheless.[15] Within our democratic system, a government's consultation policy can be a matter for debate during elections, resulting in the consultation framework varying over time.

Apart from general provincial government policy frameworks, different departments promulgate policy frameworks specific to their needs. This is the case, for example, in Saskatchewan, with the Ministry of the Environment, which is affected by the duty to consult on a daily basis. In June 2007, the Ministry adopted *Operational Procedures for Consultations with First Nations and Métis Communities*,[16] which remain in place even in the context of shifting general policy. One concern with this document is that it incorporates consultation with Aboriginal communities into the main process with other stakeholders, but this is legally permitted and may be practical so long as there continues to be respect for the full requirements of the duty to consult with Aboriginal communities.

In addition, in some instances, particular administrative bodies or decision-making boards have adopted policies in relation to how they will incorporate the consideration of Aboriginal concerns in general or the duty to consult in particular in their decision-making processes. The National Energy Board has adopted such a document,[17] as has the Ontario Energy Board.[18] These policies have adopted the filing of additional forms whereby a proponent of a project can show that it has carried out consultation and accommodation.[19] The implication of these forms, of course, is that the Ontario Energy Board will anticipate that consultation and accommodation is to be carried out largely by project proponents, rather than by governments. This is consistent with the Ontario draft consultation policy's reference to ministries "consider[ing] whether or how third parties, such as proponents or licensees, should be involved in the consultation process," also noting that "[i]n many circumstances, involving third parties in the consultation will benefit both the ministry and the Aboriginal communities."[20] This may not be consistent with the expectations of Aboriginal communities, so the Ontario draft policy recommends carefully considering Aboriginal perspectives on the consultation approach.[21]

This example illustrates a matter on which there are differences among provincial policies. Some suggest a definite place for industry stakeholders, whether through a general role as project proponents or through delegated roles within the consultation.[22] Others are clear that consultation is to be carried out only by governments.[23] The way in which the duty to consult is operationalized may differ among provincial governments on matters that are not defined within the case law, thus showing how these policies may have a significant role in defining the legal framework of consultation. Matters will, of course, be more complicated where a provincial policy on such an issue diverges from an Aboriginal community's expressed policy, a matter to which this chapter will return.

Where administrative bodies such as the National Energy Board or the Ontario Energy Board have adopted consultation policies, they have also been ready to enforce the constitutional duty to consult.[24] If there are reasonable consultation efforts under way, the National Energy Board has in some instances been quite non-interventionist, content to suggest that it "strongly supports the development of such arrangements [ongoing consultation activities and efforts to develop agreements] and encourages project proponents to build relationships with Aboriginal groups with interests in the area of their projects."[25]

Where appropriate, the National Energy Board has also been ready to scrutinize matters more closely. In February 2008, the Board released its decision in *Re Enbridge Pipelines Inc.*,[26] in which it considered an application by Enbridge concerning the construction and operation of the Alberta Clipper pipeline project. In its hearings, the National Energy Board heard from a number of Aboriginal parties, including the Standing Buffalo Dakota Nation, the Roseau River Anishinabe Nation, the Samson Cree Nation, the Maskwacis Cree Nation, the Manitoba Métis Federation, and the Montana First Nation,[27] and eventually a number of others.[28] The Board showed some reluctance to evaluate the legal adequacy of Crown consultations,[29] but was ready to consider Aboriginal interests prior to reaching a decision.[30] It was also ready to consider whether the proponent had engaged in consultation fitting with the policies enunciated by the National Energy Board, and to include conditions on approval that there be ongoing updates on consultation with Aboriginal communities, and that special rules would enter into play in the event of the finding of undiscovered historical, archæological, and burial sites.[31]

More recently, in a March 2009 decision concerning an application by SemCAMS Redwillow ULC to construct and operate a sour gas pipeline from northeastern British Columbia to facilities near Grand Prairie, Alberta,[32] the National Energy Board was ready to elaborate a substantial set of conditions and become involved in the ongoing monitoring of them. The Board was ready to direct ongoing consultation with potentially affected Aboriginal communities throughout the project's lifetime, and the filing with the Board of monthly reports during the construction phase on consultation, concerns raised, and how these were addressed.[33] Thus, in some instances, there is the potential for administrative boards and tribunals with particular expertise to enter into closer monitoring of duty to consult issues.

In some provinces, there have been moves toward embodying consultation relationships not only in policy but also in other guidelines, or even in legislation. British Columbia, facing the widest scope of Aboriginal title claims, is particularly interested in this approach. In addition to a provincial policy on consultation, a number of different government or government-associated entities have developed more specific consultation policies. These include, among others, the British Columbia Utilities Commission[34] and the Ministry of the Environment (in even such a specific context as pest management).[35] Administrative decision-making boards and tribunals have entered into considering duty to consult issues.[36] The provincial government began mooting a "New Relationship" with the province's Aboriginal peoples that included an intention to offer economic accommodation.[37]

Shortly prior to the 2009 elections, the British Columbia government was considering the possibility of legislation that would codify a number of duty to consult issues, in the form of a *Recognition and Reconciliation Act*. Aboriginal communities raised some concerns with the potential legislation, and as of this writing its fate remains unresolved. With the re-election of Gordon Campbell's government in early 2009, it will potentially move forward. Ontario does not have the same scope of Aboriginal title claims at issue, but has had some difficult history in respect of certain mining contexts, especially in contexts such as the

Platinex dispute, discussed briefly in Chapter 2. As a result, it is not surprising that it has now proposed amendments to its mining legislation designed to regularize certain elements of the duty to consult in mining contexts.[38]

The array of government policies under development or on the books is already vast. The tendency may well be toward yet more detailed policies. Policies and practices of provincial governments or ministries have become one of the important ways in which the Supreme Court of Canada's general guidance is carried into action, in the process both interpreting and adjusting that guidance to the needs of particular contexts.

4.3 Aboriginal Communities' Consultation Policies

Canadian Aboriginal communities have developed their own consultation policies in several different forms, some being at the national or provincial level and some enunciated by specific Aboriginal communities. National and provincial organizations have asserted governments' duties to consult with them at an institutional level. At the national level, the Assembly of First Nations has asserted a government obligation to consult it about legislation that might affect Aboriginal interests.[39]

Casual students of Aboriginal law often miss the complex interplay of interests at stake.[40] The duty to consult doctrine has reawakened tensions among different levels and organizations of Aboriginal representation. The *Labrador Métis Nation*[41] case marked, in some respects, an important victory for representatives of non-status and Métis communities, with the judges ready to recognize them as appropriate consultation partners. Indeed, the terms of the decision opened the possibility of consultation with representative organizations for these communities, such as the Congress of Aboriginal Peoples (CAP), which represents many non-status, Métis, and urban Aboriginal persons.[42] Apparently in response to claims by CAP, the Assembly of First Nations (AFN) has issued statements rejecting any government use of CAP for consultation purposes, illustrating some of the tension between organizations.[43] CAP's newsletter has more recently reiterated its perspective that the *Labrador Métis Nation* case is ground-breaking for the establishment of a duty to consult with CAP and its affiliated organizations where they meet conditions similar to those which the Labrador Métis Nation had met.[44]

There have also been tensions between wider organizations and their constituents. In some provinces, for instance, there have been tensions between provincial organizations and individual First Nations concerning whom the government should consult. In Saskatchewan, the Federation of Saskatchewan Indian Nations (FSIN) has engaged in the elaboration of a duty to consult policy since 2005,[45] one element being that the government would consult directly with the FSIN, implicitly in place of individual First Nations. Several First Nations' chiefs appeared at the Saskatchewan government's roundtable in May 2008 to speak against this position, asserting the ongoing need for consultation with individual First Nations, and the FSIN at the meeting backed away somewhat from its earlier position.[46] The Saskatchewan government's current duty to consult policy makes clear that it will consult directly with individual First Nations' elected representatives unless those First Nations have explicitly delegated their authority to another organization.[47] The FSIN, however, has continued to become involved in consultations, and has made applications on consultation issues in the context of administrative board hearings at which individual First Nations were already involved.[48]

In some provinces, consultation with First Nations is notably further ahead than consultation with Métis communities, owing partly to the simpler identification of legally authorized representatives of First Nations. Status Indians under the *Indian Act* have prescribed forms of representation, developed within the legislative framework and band practice. Although consulting with Aboriginal leaders under the *Indian Act* has the danger of perpetuating and extending power structures that do not necessarily correspond to traditional or desired forms of governance, the advantage for status Indians is that they have easily identified representatives for consultation purposes. Non-status Indians and Métis have already faced much neglect from governments, and the structure of the duty to consult risks reinforcing this neglect because it is not clear with whom consultation is to occur. The duty to consult may inadvertently enhance the power of already relatively advantaged Aboriginal groups over more disadvantaged ones.

The Alberta government's 2007 consultation guidelines were developed in a form that seemingly contemplates consultation with First Nations only.[49] This situation has led to provincial organizations representing Métis communities mobilizing to ensure that they will be recognized as consultation partners and trying to set out some terms of consultation relationships. In some instances they will also make applications at administrative hearings where they are concerned that project proponents have not sought to consult with Métis communities.[50] The Métis Nation of Alberta started with workshops on consultation in April 2008,[51] and has moved toward developing a consultation policy.[52] The Métis Nation of Ontario has similarly gone through community consultations in the course of developing a consultation policy.[53] The Métis Nation of Saskatchewan held a Duty to Consult conference in March 2009, seeking to develop responses to the federal and provincial policies that were open for comment at the time.[54] At least one local president urged that there be ongoing development of duty to consult policies by Métis communities themselves.[55] In the meantime, there is a Métis Nation of Saskatchewan interim policy.[56]

Although corporate and government stakeholders contacted during the writing of this book tended to identify Métis locals as what they considered the relevant consultation partner, the complex nature of Métis societies raises the risk that consultation with Métis locals alone will miss many broader issues.[57] As a result, Métis organizations have attempted to move toward regional consultation protocols. Both the Métis Nation of Ontario and the Métis Nation of British Columbia's consultation guidelines move in this direction.[58] Complex power dynamics and logistical questions are raised in the context of the duty to consult with different Aboriginal communities.

Aside from these broader developments, some individual Aboriginal communities have developed detailed consultation policies in an attempt to guide government and industry stakeholders who may need to consult with them. Many Aboriginal communities have given more specific indications on consultation issues apart from these detailed policies, with communities informing government representatives of certain consultation protocols in the course of consultation, but some communities have sought to develop more detailed policies in advance of consultation commencing. One early policy was enunciated by the Northern Shuswap Tribal Council in 2003.[59] But more detailed policies have followed in the wake of the Supreme Court of Canada trilogy.

In Alberta, the Horse Lake First Nation's Consultation Policy provides an example of an Aboriginal community setting out a relatively detailed policy concerning its expected modes of consultation.[60] The Horse Lake First Nation (HLFN) Chief and Council have authorized a representative to undertake and direct consultation processes out of the HLFN Industry Relations Corporation offices in Edmonton.[61] The HLFN Industry Relations Corporation, in turn, has offered to provide consultation expertise to other First Nations, so this policy could potentially spread more broadly. It is premised on a model of direct negotiations with government decision-makers or lead individuals in industry, as opposed to governments and industry sending agents on their behalf. Unlike the situation of other Alberta First Nations, who depend on government funding, the Horse Lake model is operated on a fee-for-service basis. The policy sets out various parameters of the Horse Lake First Nation's interpretation of the existing law on consultation, including an expectation of economic accommodation in appropriate cases.

Other First Nations have also moved toward establishing duty to consult policies. For example, Thunderchild First Nation near Turtleford, Saskatchewan, developed a Consultation Policy in July 2007, which it sent to the government and industry representatives, and established a Duty to Consult Office in August 2007.[62]

Government and industry stakeholders contacted generally suggest that they would not defer to the entirety of such policies but would, rather, follow parts of the Aboriginal communities' policies where they were not inconsistent with doctrinal law or their own policies, several suggesting that this would be for the sake of good relations with Aboriginal communities. Some provincial policies on consultation appear to suggest an even greater role for Aboriginal communities' policies where possible.[63] This degree of deference is not insignificant, but marks an accession to partial processes of Aboriginal law-making. In some instances, Aboriginal communities themselves consider the elaboration of these policies as important assertions of their rights and jurisdiction.

It remains to be tested in the courts how these policies would interact with doctrinal requirements that Aboriginal communities be engaged in good faith consultations, but the possibility that the courts will give some meaningful weight to these policies and effectively uphold Aboriginal co-jurisdiction over elements of consultation processes should not be disregarded. One existing example appears in the British Columbia Environmental Appeal Board's decision in *Xats'ull First Nation* v. *Gibraltar Mines Ltd.*,[64] in which the dissenting panel member referred to the government's failure to look at the consultation guidelines elaborated by the Xats'ull tribal council as one of the factors in her decision that the government had failed to carry out adequate consultation with the First Nation.[65] Governments obviously cannot be legally obligated to follow every measure in an Aboriginal community's consultation policy if, for instance, an Aboriginal community were to adopt a policy containing requirements not contained in the law itself. However, it would not be unreasonable to expect that governments have regard to elements of Aboriginal communities' consultation policies that are not inconsistent with the legal doctrine. To the extent that there are legal obligations to develop consultation systems collaboratively with those who are being consulted, governments might actually be obligated to do so.

Aside from any legal obligation, there are other good reasons for government and industry stakeholders to consider seriously the approaches mandated in Aboriginal communities' consultation policies. Doing so will likely promote good will and longer-term positive outcomes. Aboriginal policies will sometimes have normative force outside legal doctrine *per se*.

4.4 Development of Corporate Consultation Policies

As discussed in Chapter 2, duty to consult issues will often have major implications for corporate stakeholders as well as for governments and Aboriginal communities. This is particularly the case in the context of corporations involved in activities that need to be on certain lands, and where the sphere of their activity crosses Aboriginal traditional territories — a situation that will inevitably arise with companies involved in resource extraction and pipeline construction.[66] As a result, it is not surprising that corporations have also developed consultation policies and, in some instances, put major efforts into them. Some industry stakeholders have developed full policies, and one large resource company has established a twelve-person unit devoted to consultations. The scale of these operations should not be surprising; some corporations need to consult with dozens of Aboriginal communities in a given year. A securities filing by Talisman Energy, for instance, reports consultations with 11,500 people across five jurisdictions in relation to 1,358 projects in 2006 alone.[67]

As with governments and Aboriginal communities, the development of policies by corporations may also implicitly affect the normative framework within which the duty to consult operates. In some contexts involving the implementation of international law at national levels, corporate policies may fundamentally shape the way legal norms are applied and, indeed, involve corporations in what are, in essence, law-making processes. This phenomenon is described in the innovative work of UBC law professor Natasha Affolder, who notes that, in an international law context, "corporate engagement with treaty norms is a two-way street. Corporate behaviour can be altered by corporate interaction with these norms. But international norms can also be affected by their translation or capture by corporations."[68] Given the important role of corporate stakeholders in the duty to consult, the possibility that corporate policies and practices may be helping to shape the normative framework for the ongoing development of the duty should not be overlooked.

The development of corporate policy on the duty to consult is, of course, constrained by the size of the entities. In the context of mineral extraction, it may well be that junior exploration companies have few resources to invest in the development of duty to consult policies, whereas senior mining companies may have greater resources to do so. These differentiations may have implications for the practicalities of the doctrine and may, for instance, dictate certain approaches to when the duty to consult is considered to be triggered, as discussed in Chapter 2.

That being said, junior companies may be able to draw on industry norms and guidelines. In some instances, government departments involved in assisting industry may provide guidelines, as the Saskatchewan Mineral Exploration and Government Advisory Committee has done.[69] Government departments may provide other tools that may also be useful. For instance, Natural Resources Canada has produced a Mining Information Kit for Aboriginal Communities designed to explain a proposed exploration program to potentially affected Aboriginal communities.[70] In other instances, the pooled efforts of industry may allow for the development of policy documents. The Mining Association of Canada developed a set of guiding principles on sustainable mining and Aboriginal communities.[71] Although geared to development companies, this document represents the first phase of an industry-wide effort to establish principles to guide mine development. The Saskatchewan Mining Association, similarly, has developed a Best Management Practice to serve as a practical guide on working relations with Aboriginal communities.[72] Thus, even junior companies may be able to access legal resources without incurring the costs of developing policies on their own.

Even so, senior resource companies obviously have an advantage in the capacity they can devote to consultation initiatives. Senior companies may have developed duty to consult policies, but it would be naïve to assume that they will make these policies public. A well-developed consultation policy will, in some instances, be a competitive advantage. In speaking with industry stakeholders during the writing of this book, it became clear that, in many instances, resource companies in the same or related sector did not know whether other companies had developed duty to consult policies, and in some cases are making inaccurate guesses on the issue. As an unexpected side effect of a legal doctrine, the competition among types of enterprises may have shifted in complex ways.

Indeed, the role of the duty to consult doctrine may reshape the business landscape in favour of corporations that are able to enter into effective relationships with Aboriginal communities. Interestingly, there have been recent moves by Asian nations to enter into "nation-to-nation" discussions with Canadian Aboriginal communities with the aim of gaining access to natural resources on Aboriginal lands; Chinese and Korean investors have recently begun to put hundreds of millions of dollars into a hedge fund that will pursue related opportunities.[73] Just what these developments might mean remains to be seen.

In some instances, of course, corporate practices may be as important or more important than formalized corporate policies. Some practices will end up identifying potentially affected Aboriginal communities based on a so-called "consultation corridor" which would include Aboriginal communities within a particular distance of a pipeline right of way.[74] Following on the identification of potentially affected communities, the corporation may seek to consult only with those communities within the corridor, making it less likely that other Aboriginal communities will become involved.

In other instances, corporate practice is instantiating corporate policy in particular ways geared to negotiation with Aboriginal communities. Enbridge Inc., a major Canadian pipeline company, has featured in media reports alluding to the practice. Enbridge, which is engaged in oil pipeline expansion projects that cross traditional Dakota lands in Saskatchewan and Manitoba, negotiated a memorandum of understanding with five Dakota First Nations in Manitoba in 2007, with an extension in late 2008 leading to the payment of $100,000 to each of these First Nations.[75] Although these First Nations had originally sought intervener status at the National Energy Board hearings, they withdrew their application on signing the memorandum of understanding.[76] Enbridge also engaged in negotiation in the context of protests slowing traffic near its pipeline compound east of Regina.[77] After a week of protests, chiefs from Treaty 4 and Treaty 6 First Nations participated in a pipe ceremony with Enbridge officials to mark a confidential deal under which Enbridge apparently agreed to provide increased skills training, jobs, and contracts, as well as living allowances to some individuals in training.[78] A spokesperson for the Treaty 4 chiefs spoke of hopes for the future, saying, "We're looking at equity in future projects on this pipeline and other energy projects that Enbridge has and looking at some of their assets. We're looking at long-term revenue streams, looking at securing some of those for Treaty 6 and Treaty 4 territorial communities."[79] Corporate practices of this sort combined with Aboriginal communities' expectations may well have implications for others in that they develop practices in relation to economic accommodation or compensation.

It is possible at this stage that there are many corporate policies and practices yet to be formed or established in relation to the duty to consult. Resource companies at this stage appear to have been including only brief references on the implications of the duty to consult in their documentation to shareholders.[80] In Australia, which has a longer experience with more specific statutory norms in relation to Native title and procedural rights paralleling the duty to consult, companies have gone on to significant analysis and practice in relation to the financial, accounting, and auditing implications that arise in connection with potential Native title claims.[81] Canadian firms have yet to face these issues fully. Although some securities filings have referenced duty to consult issues,[82] there have been issues regarding limited reporting, leading in some instances to investor unrest. For example, at the May 2009 annual meeting of Enbridge Inc., one investing fund sought clarification on the risks of non-approval of the Gateway Pipeline posed by the duty to consult.[83] Many business dimensions of the duty to consult require urgent attention, but as attention is directed to these various dimensions, corporate policy and practice, which develops implicitly, says something about the expected shape of the duty to consult, shaping its form within the "law in action."

Corporate policies and practices, however, continue to develop under the influence of the duty to consult doctrine. Corporate stakeholders' policies are playing a major role in the developing "law in action" of the duty to consult, entering into engagements of conflict or coalescence with government and Aboriginal policies and practices.

4.5 Policies, Practices, and the Formation of "Law"

The specific interactions of government policies, Aboriginal communities' policies, and industry stakeholder policies open points at which there may be coalescence among the different policies. At these points of coalescence, all stakeholders may end up acting harmoniously. At points where the policies of different stakeholders diverge, there may be power-based struggles between different stakeholders, with different positions emerging at different points in time. In the absence of direct intervention by the courts, the interactions of policy may yield something amounting to "law."

A specific example may illustrate this possibility. The *Consultation Guidelines* of Alberta's provincial government specify that, "[a]s manager of the consultation process, Alberta will delegate some project-specific activities to Proponents."[84] At the same time, the *Guidelines* also acknowledge "that some First Nations have developed their own consultation protocols," and the Province "encourages, but does not require, Proponents to be aware of those protocols when consulting with First Nations."[85] Some Alberta First Nations' consultation policies, however, have indicated that they will not accept consultation with anyone other than government or the lead proponents.[86]

In an instance where Alberta attempts to delegate consultation to industry stakeholders who then attempt to consult with a First Nation that refuses to consult with them, matters will be put to the test. Each party will have to think about the possible reactions of the courts. If the First Nation refuses to consult with industry stakeholders, the courts might conclude that the government has fulfilled its duty to consult — or the courts might consider that the government has failed in that duty. It is quite possible that the parties will come to some solution in these circumstances, perhaps with government choosing not to delegate consultation in the particular situation or perhaps with the First Nation agreeing to carry out limited consultation with industry representatives. A practice that finds some way through the interstices of the different policy frameworks will create the means by which the duty to consult is carried out, thus defining the legal duty to consult through the practice of interacting stakeholders.

The particular practices that arise from initial disagreements may or may not endure, depending on whether the parties involved are willing to adapt their view to what the legal context of the duty to consult requires of them. In instances where different stakeholders are in agreement on certain practices and these are legally required — whether from the outset or through some adaptation of views — it is worth noting that the practices resulting would potentially meet requirements analogous to those required for the formation of customary international law, or perhaps customary law more generally. Consistent practice accompanied by a belief that it is legally required arguably creates a sort of customary norm, admittedly subject to alteration through other legal sources, but one that nonetheless creates a normative framework. Thus, there arises the interesting possibility that points of coalescence between these frameworks generate a sort of customary normative order.

It is not the purpose of this book to enumerate at length a new source of law. However, it is worth noting the possible development of specific forms of normative order in the context of the overarching duty, with governments, Aboriginal communities, and industry stakeholders coalescing around different needs in different parts of Canada to develop workable means of specifying the duty to consult in localized forms.

As this phenomenon develops, there may be specific reference to the policies of different organizations. Already we see that corporate policies can interact with government decision-making processes, as administrative boards will sometimes refer to corporate policies in elaborating their expectations of particular corporations.[87] We have not yet seen the citing of Aboriginal communities' policy frameworks, but, as noted earlier, in interviews it became apparent that these policies could in some instances have an impact. There may develop an interplay among the policy documents of governments, Aboriginal communities, and industry stakeholders.

David Szablowski has examined a related phenomenon in the context of interactions between Indigenous communities in developing countries, mining companies, and the World Bank.[88] He argues that the overlapping of different legal orders in a phenomenon that he calls "interlegality"[89] can lead to the constitution of a new legal order at the intersections of these legal orders and interpretations of them. The possibility that norms created in one order can create a bargaining endowment — in simpler terms, an advantage in negotiation processes — allows for a migration of norms among different orders and ultimately a legal terrain that forms from the combination of different perspectives on the relevant legal orders.[90]

4.6 Conclusion

If this chapter has in some ways seemed to be offering a long list of different policy frameworks, that has been part of its goal. The diversity of sources commenting on the duty to consult is itself significant, and illustrates the role that many people and institutions in society, beyond the courts, have in the development of the doctrine.

Roscoe Pound argues that "[i]t is the work of lawyers to make the law in action conform to the law in the books, not by futile thunderings against popular lawlessness, nor eloquent exhortations to obedience of the written law, but by making the law in the books such that the law in action can conform to it."[91] The development of different legal approaches to the duty to consult within the policies and practices of government, Aboriginal, and industry stakeholders speaks to something that is missing in the elaboration of the duty to consult doctrine by the courts. In this instance, though, it may be proper for the courts to hold back. Just as the Supreme Court of Canada is allowing the lower courts to develop elements of the doctrine in accordance with traditional common law, so, too, the courts can generally allow stakeholders to develop practices that can illuminate what is valuable in and what is challenging about the law in this area. This approach is obviously decentralizing to courts in this area, but some of the theoretical approaches to the duty to consult discussed in Chapter 1 point to how the courts see the duty to consult doctrine as a means of the courts themselves not overstepping their functional roles.

The possibility of diverse approaches within a diverse country, developed by means other than through the courts, offers the possibility of a level of detail in the doctrine that the courts have not been able to achieve in the same way. A rich body of policy and practice is emerging that can respect jurisdictional specificities, the needs of different Aboriginal communities, the economics of different industry stakeholders, and ultimately the interests of all involved. The law in action of the duty to consult is an important element of understanding the doctrine.

FIVE

∞∞∞

INTERNATIONAL AND COMPARATIVE
PERSPECTIVES FOR THE FUTURE

5.1 Introduction

The duty to consult obviously contains the seeds of its own future growth, and the examination of the case law from the lower courts in Chapters 2 and 3 has already suggested some directions in which the courts are developing the doctrine. Chapter 4 has shown how significant developments in the doctrine are also taking place outside the legal system, in the strict sense, and are being effected through the development of government policy documents, Aboriginal communities' own duty to consult policies, and corporate policies and practices related to the duty to consult. These chapters have suggested some ways in which the doctrine is evolving in response to the needs it serves.

Those needs, however, represent only some of the contexts relevant to the ongoing development of the doctrine. To the extent that the doctrine fulfills the obligations of international law in respect of Canada's treatment of Indigenous communities,[1] evolving international law standards may imply future developments of the duty to consult. To the extent that other domestic systems of consultation have grown in states that may influence Canada, particularly Australia, these approaches are worthy of consideration for what they may imply for Canada's duty to consult doctrine in future.

Chapter 6 will return to some of the theoretical perspectives on the duty to consult set out in Chapter 1 to consider them alongside the more elaborated content of the doctrine as discussed throughout the book. It will be possible to assess whether the more elaborated doctrine has implications for how those theories describe it — or their degree of "fit" with the doctrine.[2] Only with this compilation of doctrine from the lower courts, the policies and practices of various stakeholders, and the possible international and comparative influences, will it be possible to come to an understanding of the duty to consult.

5.2 International Law and the Duty to Consult

One source of future development for the duty to consult, then, is in international law. Indeed, the Canadian approach to the duty to consult is situated within the context of a larger set of international law norms on the rights of Indigenous peoples, and these norms have important interactions with the Canadian duty to consult doctrine.

Recent decades have featured a major international effort by Indigenous peoples worldwide to have their rights as Indigenous peoples recognized by an international legal system that has, by the state-centred nature of international law, tended to exclude them from consideration.[3] This effort has recently culminated in the adoption by the United Nations General Assembly of the *Declaration on the Rights of Indigenous Peoples*.[4] This was not accomplished without controversy; indeed, it took over a decade of negotiation from the draft text and came close to facing a sharply divided vote in the General Assembly.[5] In the end, the *Declaration* passed the General Assembly by a vote of 143 votes to 4, but with 11 abstentions and 36 absences.[6] Many of the abstentions and absences were African states that likely had ongoing concerns with the *Declaration*.[7] The four votes against were settler states of particular significance within the Anglo-American legal world: Australia, New Zealand, the United States, and Canada.[8] On this last point, more recently, Australia has taken steps under a new government to indicate its assent.[9] There are also indications that the Obama administration in the United States will take a different tack than its predecessor; some representatives have indicated that the issue is under review, and campaigns are under way to urge the President to endorse the

Declaration. There have been some recent suggestions that New Zealand, too, might back the *Declaration*; Radio New Zealand reported on May 17, 2009 that Prime Minister John Key's administration could eventually endorse the *Declaration*, although its endorsement would be subject to some caveats.[10] In this, New Zealand would join the forty states — an unusually large number — that chose to make interventions explaining or qualifying their votes in the United Nations. For certain technical reasons, it is at this stage unclear whether the *Declaration* represents the current state of international law, but its adoption nonetheless indicates a vibrant area of international law to which close attention is warranted.

The *Declaration*, in many respects, continued the development of already developing norms, and this is true to some degree in respect of obligations of consultation with Indigenous peoples. Prior to the broader UN process associated with the *Declaration*, the International Labour Organization engaged in a process of attempting to delineate certain international law obligations in respect of Indigenous peoples, culminating in ILO Convention No. 169 of 1989.[11] This Convention, which attracted a limited number of signatories but is nonetheless illustrative of developing international law, set forth two consultation-related obligations whose form carries forward into the UN's *Draft Declaration* of 1994 and the *Declaration* as ultimately adopted in 2007. In respect of obligations under the ILO Convention, the Convention commits in Article 6:

1. In applying the provisions of this Convention, Governments shall:

    (a) Consult the peoples concerned, through appropriate procedures and in particular through their representative institutions, whenever consideration is being given to legislative or administrative measures which may affect them directly;

    (b) Establish means by which these peoples can freely participate, to at least the same extent as other sectors of the population, at all levels of decision-making in elective institutions and administrative and other bodies responsible for policies and programmes which concern them;

    (c) Establish means for the full development of these peoples' own institutions and initiatives, and in appropriate cases provide the resources necessary for this purpose.

2. The consultations carried out in application of this Convention shall be undertaken, in good faith and in a form appropriate to the circumstances, with the objective of achieving agreement or consent to the proposed measures.[12]

A second, more specific duty arises in relation to resources, as set out in Article 15(2) of the ILO Convention:

In cases in which the State retains the ownership of mineral or sub-surface resources or rights to other resources pertaining to lands, governments shall establish or maintain procedures through which they shall consult these peoples, with a view to ascertaining whether and to what degree their interests would be prejudiced, before undertaking or permitting any programmes for the exploration or exploitation of such resources pertaining to their lands. The peoples concerned shall wherever possible participate in the benefits of such activities, and shall receive fair compensation for any damages which they may sustain as a result of such activities.

These provisions appeared in stronger terms in Articles 20 and 30 of the *Draft Declaration* of 1994. Article 20 provided:

Indigenous peoples have the right to participate fully, if they so choose, through procedures determined by them, in devising legislative or administrative measures that may affect them. States shall obtain the free and informed consent of the peoples concerned before adopting and implementing such measures.

Article 30 provided:

Indigenous peoples have the right to determine and develop priorities and strategies for the development or use of their lands, territories and other resources, including the right to require that States obtain their free and informed consent prior to the approval of any project affecting their lands, territories and other resources, particularly in connection with the development, utilization or exploitation of mineral, water or other resources. Pursuant to agreement with the indigenous peoples concerned, just and fair compensation shall be provided for any such activities and measures taken to mitigate adverse environmental, economic, social, cultural, or spiritual impact.

These provisions are somewhat moderated before the final form of the *Declaration* in 2007, but they do appear in a similar form in Articles 18, 19, and 32 of the *Declaration,* where signatories commit to consultation that is to obtain "free, prior, and informed consent" (sometimes called FPIC) of Indigenous peoples in a number of contexts:

18 Indigenous peoples have the right to participate in decision-making in matters which would affect their rights, through representatives chosen by themselves in accordance with their own procedures, as well as to maintain and develop their own indigenous decision-making institutions.

19 States shall consult and co-operate in good faith with the indigenous peoples concerned through their own representative institutions in order to obtain their free, prior and informed consent before adopting and implementing legislative or administrative measures that may affect them.

32 (1) Indigenous peoples have the right to determine and develop priorities and strategies for the development or use of their lands or territories and other resources.

(2) States shall consult and co-operate in good faith with the indigenous peoples concerned through their own representative institutions in order to obtain their free and informed consent prior to the approval of any project affecting their lands or territories and other resources, particularly in connection with the development, utilization or exploitation of mineral, water or other resources.

(3) States shall provide effective mechanisms for just and fair redress for any such activities, and appropriate measures shall be taken to mitigate adverse environmental, economic, social, cultural or spiritual impact.

Some read the FPIC components of the *Declaration* as subject to its general balancing provisions, notably those contained in Article 46(2):

> The exercise of the rights set forth in this Declaration shall be subject only to such limitations as are determined by law and in accordance with international human rights obligations. Any such limitations shall be non-discriminatory and strictly necessary solely for the purpose of securing due recognition and respect for the rights and freedoms of others and for meeting the just and most compelling requirements of a democratic society.

Canada's official representatives saw elements of the *Declaration* as more worrisome, significantly influencing Canada's decision to vote against it. Canada's reasons for opposition arose partly from the effects of the *Declaration* text in the context of the matters at stake relating to the duty to consult. The UN press release notes that John McNee, Canada's Ambassador to the United Nations, assured the General Assembly of Canada's ongoing strong support for Aboriginal rights, but indicated concerns with the Declaration:

> [S]ome of the provisions dealing with the concept of free, prior and informed consent were unduly restrictive, he said. Provisions in the Declaration said that States could not act on any legislative or administrative matter that might affect indigenous peoples without obtaining their consent. While Canada had a strong consultative process, reinforced by the Courts as a matter of law, the establishment of complete veto power over legislative action for a particular group would be fundamentally incompatible with Canada's parliamentary system.[13]

The uncertain relationship between the Canadian doctrine of the duty to consult and the consultation requirements contained in international law could give rise to different interpretations. Prior to the adoption of the final form of the *Declaration*, James Anaya, a leading scholar on Indigenous rights in international law, had already argued that "[t]he provisions of Convention No. 169 and the draft declarations . . . represent a consensus that extends well beyond states that have ratified Convention No. 169 or the authorized experts that developed the drafts."[14] Anaya made other points specifically in relation to provisions on participation and consultation, noting, for instance, that the World Bank had taken on these concerns in its operational policies, and concluding, from states' comments, that "[i]t is evident that there exists a broad acceptance of minimum requirements of consultation among states and others participating in the discussions on these drafts, even while certain disagreement persists about the particular wording that should make its way into the final declarations."[15] One could interpret this consensus as continuing through the formulation of the final *Declaration*, which obviously gained the assent of more states.

Such an analysis would situate Canada's duty to consult doctrines at the heart of an ongoing development of state practice within the international order, both contributing to and engaged with the norms developing within the international order in relation to Indigenous peoples. Canadian Aboriginal leaders have sought to link the duty to consult doctrine to this larger framework,[16] as have some government documents.[17] Emerging international norms have been persuasive to courts as well, with, for example, the Supreme Court of Canada having referred to some provisions of the *Draft Declaration* in its case law.[18]

To the extent that the wording on "free, prior, and informed consent" in the *Declaration* meets with significant agreement in the international community, it might be seen as reflecting an evolving norm of international law that might influence the future shape of the Canadian duty to consult doctrine. At the moment, however, one would likely also be right to see the Canadian duty to consult doctrine as part of the international law norm requiring some minimum degree of consultation with Indigenous peoples. Canada's doctrine is part of, and engaged with, international norms on relationships with Indigenous peoples. The evolution of international law in this area may have future impacts on the Canadian doctrine.

5.3 Comparative Law: Australia's Experience with the "Right to Negotiate"

Given the trend toward transnational legal dialogue in various spheres — an enormous phenomenon in recent years — a second plausible source of impact on Canada's duty to consult is contained in other domestic legal orders with analogous doctrines. In her judgment in *Haida Nation*, McLachlin C.J.C. refers to an early New Zealand document on consultation with the Maori,[19] illustrating the interest in comparative perspectives. One legal system of particular interest in this respect is that of Australia, which contrasts significantly with the somewhat general and even vague tone of international law in that it offers a rather detailed statutory framework of interest. Comparative considerations of the Canadian duty to consult doctrine have not attracted much consideration to date, despite the judicial references to New Zealand consultation documents discussed in *Haida Nation* — one notable exception being a 2005 paper by Daniel Guttman on "Australian and Canadian Approaches to Native Title,"[20] The lack of discussion on the issue is somewhat surprising, given the level of interest by Australians in Canadian Aboriginal title cases such as *Delgamuukw*, and Canadian interest in the Australian decision in *Mabo and Others* v. *Queensland (No 2)*,[21] a landmark case rejecting a prior concept of *terra nullius* — "land belonging to no-one"— and making way for the recognition of a form of Native title.[22] This lack of attention to comparative experiences of consultation is unfortunate, for the Australian system has a particular salience for Canada that is not present in every attempt at comparative law in the Indigenous rights context.

Australia's consultation system has developed differently from the Canadian duty to consult doctrine in that Australia's law in this area arises less from judicial decisions than from statutory norms. That being said, the development of the law was certainly prompted by judicial decisions, particularly the Australian High Court's decision in *Mabo*.[23] Following that decision, Australia chose to adopt a legislative framework on Aboriginal title in an attempt to clarify the area more rapidly than would have occurred through ongoing judicial development, and the government adopted the *Native Title Act, 1993*,[24] which entered into force on January 1, 1994. Following the next landmark decision of the High Court, *Wik Peoples* v. *Queensland*,[25] difficult debates ensued, and the government adopted major amendments to the statutory framework in 1998.[26]

A significant component of Australia's legislative framework is the "right to negotiate" arising in relation to "future acts." The basic norm to this effect is found in subs. 25(2) of the *Native Title Act, 1993*: "Before the future act is done, the parties must negotiate with a view to reaching an agreement about the act." In relation to proposed government actions of certain types (especially mining-related grants and title-related grants to a third party), a compulsory negotiation process commences between the government, the third party beneficiary, and registered Native title holders and claimants.[27] There is a period in which negotiation is to occur, and, if that is unsuccessful, then matters go to the National Native Title Tribunal for adjudication on whether the action can go ahead and on what conditions.[28]

Pursuant to room in the Australian Commonwealth legislation for the development of state legislation, the Australian state of Queensland has chosen to develop its own right to negotiate framework in directions different than those chosen by the Commonwealth government, so as to offer greater clarity in the context of the state's mining industry.[29] The Queensland framework creates a two-tiered system, with low-impact exploration activities giving rise to a simpler regime of notification and consultation, and higher-impact mining activities giving rise to a larger right to negotiate.[30] The Queensland system is intended to be more applicant-driven, with the applicant for mining rights to which the high-impact system applies launching the process and assuming the greater responsibility for it.[31] It is also intended to refer stalled cases to a state-based Land and Resources Tribunal that will not have the backlog faced by the National Native Title Tribunal, with the hope of this speeding up the process.[32] The framework is much more detailed than this description, but this hopefully gives some sense of it.

Within a framework developing a procedural right paralleling the duty to consult through statute, Australia's governments have become engaged in the development of detailed procedures, particularly to try to balance the complex needs of resource extraction industries with the rights of Australia's Indigenous communities. Similarly detailed processes cannot arise as readily, or as systematically, from the development of the Canadian duty to consult through case law. That said, the statutory option is not obviously present in the Canadian context. Particularly in relation to resource industries, where provinces have strongly taken jurisdictional authority since the 1982 constitutional amendments, the federal government would face a difficult division of powers barrier in enacting legislation to clarify the duty to consult.[33] At the same time, the overriding federal jurisdiction in relation to Aboriginal communities, particularly Aboriginal title or rights,[34] would render it difficult for a province to enact legislation to clarify the duty to consult through statutory norms. Though there might be ways around this division-of-powers Catch-22 — British Columbia presumably believes it has found some (see discussion in Chapter 4) — the more probable course will be ongoing elaboration of provincial policy rather than legislation, and the establishment of practices at the interaction points of government, corporate, and Aboriginal policies.

The Australian example does illustrate how some of the same issues that have been challenging in Canada have been subject to different legislative consideration. The issue of the role of applicant corporations seeking to explore or develop particular resources would have been a matter for different consideration under the Queensland framework than under the national framework. Those developing Canadian policies and practice are well advised to be carefully attuned to the needs in particular areas and sectors for larger governmental or industry roles.

Australia's system has a fundamental route around its right-to-negotiate system with the possibility of negotiated "Indigenous Land Use Agreements."[35] Such agreements, once they make it through a registration process, bind all Native title holders in a certain area.[36] If mining companies can identify correctly the relevant Native title parties and develop friendly relationships that foster win-win solutions, they may effectively negotiate around the right-to-negotiate system. One challenge of this approach is that it does involve time and a meaningful commitment of resources to both relationships and negotiations. Partly for these reasons, some industry stakeholders in Canada are tending to avoid the prospect of entering into separate negotiations outside the duty to consult framework, although the possibility would seemingly exist in Canada as well, at least in part. By the right form of negotiated agreement, Aboriginal rights holders could agree not to pursue certain kinds of Aboriginal rights claims or claims based on the duty to consult versus particular developments. However, the Canadian system, without a registration procedure for such agreements — which would need to be developed through the kind of legislation discussed above — would give rise to several problems. First, if a company negotiating an agreement did not correctly identify the possible parties, the consequences would be more serious, being not just the non-registration of the agreement, but presumably its continuing effect with some Aboriginal communities and its ultimate invalidity *vis-à-vis* others. Second, such an agreement would not remove the Crown's duty to consult, so would not remove all delays resulting therefrom. Nonetheless, the possibility exists for such agreements to develop through Canadian practice. Indeed, some larger companies, some with dozens of staff in their Aboriginal engagement and consultation departments, might gain a competitive advantage through their ongoing development of relationships and their negotiation of agreements in advance of foreseen future developments. Australia's framework illustrates certain possibilities for development in the Canadian context.

Australia's framework also demonstrates how the procedural rights created within one system can establish bargaining strength that communities may try to "trade" for substantive outcomes within other rights systems — namely, those concerned with substantive rights connected with Native title or compensatory frameworks. Thus, there have been attempts by representatives in Australia to "trade" procedural negotiation rights for compensation related to the value of minerals at issue, such as through obtaining royalty rights.[37] This mode of compensation does not entirely match the valuation methods within the Australian legislation, which is concerned more with the effect on the Indigenous community as the background legal condition — although allowing for negotiation of profit-sharing in some circumstances[38] — but it may nonetheless become a practicable mode for those paying compensation in the context of certain resource developments, partly because it is a gradual mode of payment occurring alongside future output.[39] However, gradual payments also contain the danger of future disputes for resource companies.[40] Moreover, any transition to such compensation systems may exert pressures on other contexts, even internationally, as networks of advocates become aware of solutions developed in other contexts. Canadian resource companies faced with such possibilities will find themselves in complex and difficult situations, particularly if a company can gain a competitive advantage by launching a compensation system beyond the legal rights discussed in Chapter 3, but in doing so possibly alter the compensation frameworks for others in the future.

Aboriginal communities, of course, have every reason to press for such possibilities, particularly as they become more aware of elements of the Australian experience. As discussed in Chapter 4, many Aboriginal communities have been pushing for compensatory frameworks in the context of the duty to consult. Informed in part by comparative legal experience, the ultimate shape of the doctrine in action will depend on ongoing negotiations.

5.4 Conclusion

Whatever Canada does in terms of the duty to consult, it does not act in "splendid isolation." Our relationship with Indigenous peoples exists in the context of a set of developing international norms. Along with norms developed in specific comparative contexts, our approach becomes an instance of state practice in the ongoing development of these norms. Although some claims concerning the contents of international law are less certain than they might first appear, it is nonetheless the case that international law may affect the future development of Canada's duty to consult doctrine. Our doctrine may also be affected by comparative doctrine in other countries, such as Australia, which is facing similar questions. The duty to consult doctrine is not static but contains potential for ongoing growth.

ooooo

UNDERSTANDING
THE DUTY TO CONSULT

THIS BOOK HAS ATTEMPTED A NUMBER OF THINGS. Chapter 1 introduced
the modern duty to consult doctrine and set out a number of possible theoretical approaches to understanding it. Chapters 2 and 3 set out a number
of doctrinal parameters on the doctrine as it has developed, with Chapter
2 dealing with legal parameters such as the triggering conditions and who
is involved in a consultation, and Chapter 3 dealing with the content of a
consultation. Chapter 4 showed the ways in which the lower court case
law behind Chapters 2 and 3 has left room for the development of much
more policy and practice by governments, Aboriginal communities, and
industry stakeholders that is seeing the doctrine develop in further ways.
Chapter 5 showed some possible future influences on the doctrine so far
as it is rooted in, engaged in, and subject to influence from transnational
components in international and comparative law.

In some senses, the aim of understanding the duty to consult would now
arguably call for assessing which of the theoretical models mentioned in
Chapter 1 has the best "fit" with the doctrine as developed through lower
court judgments discussed in Chapters 2 and 3, with the "law in action" as

developed in Chapter 4, and with the evolving possibilities of international and comparative law in Chapter 5. In other senses, this might look like a problematic task, for the nature of what has gone on in the context of the duty to consult features many moves arising from power relations or from what appears to work in particular circumstances.

In terms of the theoretical approaches of Chapter 1, the duty to consult is about a relationship between the Crown and Aboriginal peoples, and might be thought of in terms of honourable relationships, but the duty to consult is about more than this. It is about the ways in which government stakeholders, Aboriginal stakeholders, corporate stakeholders, and ultimately all Canadians can co-exist in ways living out honour while allowing for the development of new futures. To describe the duty to consult in terms of the honour of the Crown would be to describe something about it, but much less than what it can be.

The duty to consult is about fostering negotiation processes and ensuring that actions that take place in advance of concluded negotiations or judicial decisions will not be to the unreasonable detriment of Aboriginal stakeholders. There are contexts where this element is central to the duty to consult, but they can involve a defensive conception of it where there are also much richer ways in which it is developing. The duty to consult is about an economically efficient means of addressing issues, rather than using the set of injunctions that the full array of Aboriginal rights and title claims could generate. But it is far from solely an economic doctrine. The duty to consult may in some instances be a vehicle of reconciliation or the generation of new norms that further it, but the doctrinal limits on it also make it a limited vehicle for pursuing those aims in some circumstances.

There is a deeply pragmatic sense to the way in which the duty to consult has developed. Much of the doctrine and policy is related to what will work. At the same time, many doctrinal decisions indicate a deep rootedness in principle, with the underlying principles of the duty to consult helping to determine previously unresolved questions on the doctrine.

When courts make determinations on these questions in the coming years, I would suggest in the end that it would be a mistake to choose just one underlying principle for the doctrine. It is a complex doctrine that embodies a number of related aims and aspirations that give rise to various principles related to it. It has room to grow in these principled ways and in localized ways that work. To cut off the doctrine in narrow ways at this stage would be to do it a disservice.

Admittedly, this approach leaves lingering uncertainties about some matters. However, the doctrine in its current form is but five years old. No area of the common law has ever crystallized in a mere five years. There will be ongoing development in the duty to consult, and this is an exciting, enriching element of a diverse Canada.

1   *Constitution Act, 1982*, s. 35, being Schedule B to the *Canada Act, 1982* (U.K.) 1982, c. 11. This book presumes a basic understanding of s. 35, which states that "existing aboriginal and treaty rights of the aboriginal peoples of Canada are hereby recognized and affirmed." Misunderstandings of s. 35 sometimes plague discussions of the duty to consult.

2   *Seeking Common Ground: Roundtable Conference on First Nations and Métis Consultation and Accommodation: Conference Report* (Regina: Government of Saskatchewan Ministry of First Nations and Métis Relations, 2008) at 5: www.fnmr.gov.sk.ca/roundtable-conference-report.

3   *R. v. Sparrow*, [1990] 1 S.C.R. 1075, 70 D.L.R. (4th) 385.

4   *Haida Nation* v. *British Columbia (Minister of Forests)* 2004 SCC 73, [2004] 3 S.C.R. 511.

5   *Taku River Tlingit First Nation* v. *British Columbia (Project Assessment Director)* 2003 SCC 74, [2004] 3 S.C.R. 550.

6   *Mikisew Cree First Nation* v. *Canada (Minister of Canadian Heritage)* 2005 SCC 69, [2005] 3 S.C.R. 388.

7   In some cases, consultation requirements may be determined by the terms of particular agreements rather than the general constitutional doctrine. The *Nisga'a Final Agreement* (27 Apr. 1999), for example, establishes consultation requirements on federal and provincial regulations or policies affecting wildlife and bird management in the Nass Valley (9:50, 9:53, 9:95, and 9:96), and on provincial decisions on traplines and guiding (9:76, 9:82, and 9:85): www.ainc-inac.gc.ca/al/ldc/ccl/fagr/nsga/nis/nis-eng.asp. The *Tlicho Agreement* (25 Aug. 2003) also contains numerous provisions on consultation (see especially 7.5.5, 7.13.5, 10.7.1, 12.5.1, 12.5.11, 12.12.1, 13.2.1, 14.3.2, 14.5.1, 15.1.5, 16.6.1, 17.2.7(b), 17.5.5, 21.4.2, 22.2.13, 23.2, 23.3, 23.6, 25.2, and 26.3.): http://www.collectionscanada.gc.ca/webarchives/20071124232758/http://www.ainc-inac.gc.ca/pr/agr/nwts/tliagr2_e.pdf. However, as the Yukon Court of Appeal stated in its Aug. 2008 decision in *Little Salmon/Carmacks First Nation* v. *Yukon (Minister of Energy, Mines, and Resources)*, "a duty to consult and accommodate applies in the interpretation of treaties and exists independent of treaties." Kirkpatrick J.A., considering a government argument that the "certainty clause" in the *Little Salmon/Carmacks Final Agreement* made clear that the agreement was intended to specify duties of consultation and thus precluded constitutional duties to consult on matters covered within the agreement affirmed that the constitutional duty to consult applies independently of the terms of a negotiated agreement.

8   Notable exceptions include: Patrick Macklem & Sonia Lawrence, "From Consultation to Reconciliation: Aboriginal Rights and the Crown's Duty to Consult" (2000) 79 Can. Bar Rev. 252; Thomas Isaac & Anthony Knox, "The Crown's Duty to Consult Aboriginal People" (2003) 41 Alta. L. Rev. 49; Jeffrey Harris, "Emerging Issues: Natural Resources and the Duty to Consult and Accommodate: An Examination of the Content," in *Proceedings of the National Aboriginal Law CLE Conference* (Ottawa: Canadian Bar Association, Mar. 2005); Ronalda Murphy, Richard Devlin & Tamara Lorincz, "Aquaculture Law and Policy in Canada and the Duty to Consult with Aboriginal Peoples," in David L. VanderZwaag & Gloria Chao (Eds.), *Aquaculture Law and Policy: Towards Principled Access and Operations* (New York: Routledge, 2006), p. 293; Heather L. Treacy, Tara L. Campbell & Jamie D. Dickson, "The Current State of the Law on Crown Obligations to Consult and Accommodate Aboriginal Interests in Resource Development" (2007) 44 Alta. L. Rev. 571; Maria Morellato, "The Crown's Constitutional Duty to Consult and Accommodate Aboriginal and Treaty Rights," National Centre for First Nations Governance Research Paper (Feb. 2008).

9   *Haida Nation, supra* note 4 at paras. 34-38.

10   See especially *Halfway River First Nation* v. *British Columbia (Minister of Forests)* (1999) 64 B.C.L.R. (3d) 206 (B.C.C.A.).

11   *Sparrow, supra* note 3 at para. 67 .

12   *Haida Nation, supra* note 4 at para. 53.

13   *Ibid.,* at paras. 53-56; *Haida Nation* v. *British Columbia (Minister of Forests)* 2002 BCCA 462, 216 D.L.R. (4th) 1 at para. 73.

14   *Haida Nation, supra* note 4 at para. 53; *Taku River Tlingit, supra* note 5 at paras. 18, 46.

Notes to Chapter One

1   *Haida Nation* v. *British Columbia (Minister of Forests)* 2004 SCC 73, [2004] 3 S.C.R. 511.

2   *Ibid.,* at paras. 31, 32, 76.

3   *Ibid.,* at para. 35.

4   *Ibid.,* at paras. 43-45.

5   *Ibid.,* at para. 53.

6   *Ibid.,* at paras. 76, 79.

7   *Taku River Tlingit First Nation* v. *British Columbia (Project Assessment Director)* 2003 SCC 74, [2004] 3 S.C.R. 550.

8   *Ibid.*, at paras. 22, 47.

9   *Ibid.*, at para. 32.

10   *Ibid.*, at para. 41.

11   *Mikisew Cree First Nation* v. *Canada (Minister of Canadian Heritage)* 2005 SCC 69, [2005] 3 S.C.R. 388.

12   *Ibid.*, at paras. 63, 32-34, 51-56.

13   *Ibid.*, at para. 3.

14   *Ibid.*, at para. 59.

15   *Ibid.*, at para. 69.

16   *Ibid.*, at para. 67.

17   *Ibid.*, at para. 34.

18   *Ibid.*, at paras. 33, 44.

19   See: Kent McNeil, *Common Law Aboriginal Title* (Oxford: Clarendon, 1989); and Brian Slattery, "Understanding Aboriginal Rights" (1987) 66 Can. Bar Rev. 727. Slattery offers a powerful conception of the nature of Aboriginal rights as arising intersocietally from the onset of encounter among different communities.

20   See Dwight G. Newman, "You Still Know Nothin' 'Bout Me: Toward Cross-Cultural Theorizing of Aboriginal Rights" (2007) 52 McGill L.J. 725.

21   For an interesting discussion of the shifts in Aboriginal title jurisprudence, see Kent McNeil, "Aboriginal Title and the Supreme Court: What's Happening?" (2006) 69 Sask. L. Rev. 281; see also Dwight G. Newman, "Prior Occupation and Schismatic Principles: Toward a Normative Theorization of Aboriginal Title" (2007) 44 Alta. L. Rev. 779.

22   This description of the content of the law is coherent with Ronald Dworkin's *Taking Rights Seriously* (London: Duckworth, 1978). Dworkin has in more recent works offered a more extended account, suggesting that decision-making in each particular case must consider the two elements of a decision's fit with existing jurisprudence and its moral soundness, thus bridging positivism's close definition of legal content and natural law's emphasis on the justness of law. See Dworkin's *Law's Empire* (Cambridge: Belknap, 1986) and *Justice in Robes* (Cambridge: Harvard University Press, 2006).

23   See, for example, *Haida Nation, supra* note 1 at para. 16.

24　Roger Earl of Rutland's Case (1608) 8 Co. Rep. 55a at 56a-b, 77 E.R. 555 at 557; the Case of the Churchwardens of St. Saviour in Southwark (1613) 10 Co. Rep. 66b a 67b, 77 E.R. 1025 at 1027.

25　*Haida Nation, supra* note 1 at paras. 35-36; *Mikisew Cree First Nation, supra* note 11 at paras. 33-34.

26　*Haida Nation, supra* note 1 at para. 35.

27　*Haida Nation, supra* note 1 at paras. 43-45; *Taku River Tlingit First Nation, supra* note 7 at para. 32.

28　*Haida Nation, supra* note 1 at para. 48.

29　*Ibid.*, at paras. 13-14.

30　*Ibid.*, at para. 16.

31　*Ibid.*, at paras. 19-20.

32　*Ibid.*, at para. 14.

33　The term originates with Robert H. Mnookin & Lewis Kornhauser, "Bargaining in the Shadow of the Law: The Case of Divorce" (1979) 88 Yale L.J. 950.

34　See Dwight G. Newman, "Negotiated Rights Enforcement" (2006) 69 Sask. L. Rev. 119.

35　*Ibid.*

36　Just to be clear at this juncture, I do speak of the doctrine only as enunciated in *Haida Nation*. Some lower courts have been more ready to apply internal limits to when the duty to consult is triggered.

37　Dwight Newman, "Reconciliation: Legal Conception(s) and Faces of Justice," in John Whyte (Ed.), *Moving Toward Justice* (Saskatoon: Purich, 2008).

38　*Haida Nation, supra* note 1 at para. 26.

39　See also the statement of Phelan J. in *Dene Tha' First Nation v. Canada (Minister of Environment)* 2006 FC 1354 [2007] 1 C.N.L.R. 1 at para. 82, aff'd, 2008 FCA 20, 378 N.R. 251: "The goal of consultation is not to be narrowly interpreted as the mitigation of adverse effects on Aboriginal rights and/or title" (going on to state that the underlying goal of the doctrine is reconciliation).

40　One could argue, for example, that honourable dealings will best promote reconciliation and thus arrive back at the first theory. That said, such moves might not seem the most plausible. There is a difference in orientation between asking the government to act in accord with a virtue of honour and asking the government to act in accord with a value of reconciliation.

41　Brian Slattery, "Aboriginal Rights and the Honour of the Crown" (2005) 29 S.C.L.R. (2d) 433, and "The Generative Structure of Aboriginal Rights" (2007) 38 S.C.L.R. (2d) 1.

42　Slattery, "Aboriginal Rights and the Honour of the Crown," *ibid.*, at 440.

43　*Haida Nation*, *supra* note 1 at para. 32, cited by Slattery, *ibid.*

44　Some of this suggestion was present in the recent trial court decision in *Tsilhqot'in Nation* v. *British Columbia*, 2007 BCSC 1700, [2008] 1 C.N.L.R. 112, 163 A.C.W.S. (3d) 873. For discussion, see Dwight Newman & Danielle Schweitzer, "Between Reconciliation and the Rule(s) of Law: *Tsilhqot'in Nation* v. *British Columbia*" (2008) 42 U.B.C. L. Rev. 249. The *Tsilhqot'in Nation* trial judgment's uncertainties around private property issues have already influenced a recent duty to consult decision in *Hupacasath First Nation* v. *British Columbia (Minister of Forests)* 2008 BCSC 1505, [2009] 1 C.N.L.R. 30.

NOTES TO CHAPTER TWO

1　*Haida Nation* v. *British Columbia (Minister of Forests)* [2004] 3 S.C.R. 511, 2004 SCC 73 at para. 11.

2　*Carrier Sekani Tribal Council* v. *British Columbia (Utilities Commission)* 2009 BCCA 67 at para. 1; leave to appeal to SCC requested 33132 (17 Apr. 2009).

3　*R.* v. *Lefthand*, 2007 ABCA 206, 77 Alta. L.R. (4th) 203 at para. 37; leave to appeal to SCC refused 385 N.R. 392 (21 Feb. 2008).

4　*Haida Nation*, *supra* note 1 at paras. 34-37; *Mikisew Cree First Nation* v. *Canada (Minister of Canadian Heritage)* 2005 SCC 69, [2005] 3 S.C.R. 388 at para. 34.

5　*Haida Nation*, *supra* note 1 at para. 35.

6　*Mikisew Cree First Nation*, *supra* note 4 at para. 34.

7　*Haida Nation*, *supra* note 1 at para. 36.

8　*Ibid.*, at para. 37.

9　*Ibid.*

10　*Cf. Mikisew Cree First Nation*, *supra* note 4 at para. 25.

11　*Osoyoos Indian Band* v. *Oliver (Town)* [2001] 3 S.C.R. 746, 2001 SCC 85 at paras. 41-43.

12　*Haida Nation*, *supra* note 1 at paras. 35-36; *R* v. *Bernard*, [2005] 2 S.C.R. 220, 2005 SCC 43 at para. 25.

13   See, generally, *R. v. Van der Peet*, [1996] 2 S.C.R. 507, 137 D.L.R. (4th) 289.

14   See, for example, *Acadia Band* v. *M.N.R.*, 2008 FCA 119, [2008] C.N.L.R. 17 at paras. 4-5.

15   *Van der Peet, supra* note 13.

16   *R. v. Sappier; R. v. Gray*, [2006] 2 S.C.R. 686, 2006 SCC 54 at paras. 42-49.

17   *Mikisew Cree First Nation, supra* note 4 at para. 34.

18   *Ibid.*, at paras. 33-34.

19   *Ibid.*, at para. 55.

20   *Haida Nation, supra* note 1 at para. 37.

21   *Mikisew Cree First Nation, supra* note 4 at para. 33.

22   2007 FC 45, [2007] 2 C.N.L.R. 233, 71 Admin. L.R. (4th) 1 at paras. 68-70.

23   *Native Council of Nova Scotia v. Canada*, 2008 FCA 113, 165 A.C.W.S. (3d) 1, [2008] 3 C.N.L.R. 286 at para. 5.

24   *Ahousaht Indian Band* v. *Canada (Minister of Fisheries & Oceans)* 2008 FCA 212, 297 D.L.R. (4th) 722.

25   *Ibid.*, at paras. 36-37. See also *Acadia Band* v. *Canada* (M.N.R.) *supra* note 14 at para. 10.

26   See *Labrador Métis Nation* v. *Newfoundland and Labrador (Minister of Transportation and Works)* 2007 NLCA 75, 288 D.L.R. (4th) 641 at paras. 36-45, 50-51 (citing *Haida Nation*'s reference at *supra* note 1, paras. 37-38 to a "preliminary evidence-based assessment of the strength of the claim"); leave to appeal to SCC refused 32468 (29 May 2008).

27   *Haida Nation, supra* note 1 at para. 35.

28   *R. v. Douglas*, 2007 BCCA 265, 278 D.L.R. (4th) 263; leave to appeal to SCC refused 383 N.R. 382 (15 Nov. 2007).

29   *Ibid.*, at para. 44.

30   *Ibid.*

31   *Supra* note 3.

32   *Ibid.*, at para. 38.

33   *Ibid.*, at para. 126.

34   *Haida Nation, supra* note 1 at paras. 27, 33.

35   *Labrador Métis Nation, supra* note 26 at paras. 4, 29, 227.

36   *Ibid.*, at paras. 24, 29. See also *Ochapowace First Nation (Indian Band No. 71)* v. *Canada (Attorney General)* 2009 FCA 124 at para. 37, suggesting that the exercise of police discretion is also in a realm outside the application of the duty to consult.

37   *Paul First Nation* v. *Parkland (County)* 2006 ABCA 128, [2006] C.N.L.R. 243, at paras. 7, 12.

38   *Tsuu T'ina First Nation* v. *Alberta (Environment)* (2008) 96 Alta. L.R. (4th) 65, 2008 ABQB 547 at paras. 57-59.

39   *Ibid.*, at para. 59, citing *Lefthand, supra* note 3.

40   *Lefthand, supra* note 3 at para. 38.

41   *Ibid.*, at para. 194.

42   *Dene Tha' First Nation* v. *Canada (Minister of Environment)* 2006 FC 1354, [2007] 1 C.N.L.R. 1 [*Dene Tha'* (Fed. Ct.)], aff'd 2008 FCA 20, 378 N.R. 251.

43   *Dene Tha'* (Fed. Ct.) *supra* note 42 at para. 100.

44   *Ibid.*, at para. 106.

45   *Ibid.*, at para. 106, citing *Haida Nation, supra* note 1 at para. 76.

46   I am indebted to Mitch McAdam for drawing this issue to my attention. He discussed the issue in a Saskatchewan Legal Education Society presentation, "Duty to Consult and Accommodate Aboriginal and Treaty Rights: A Practical Guide for Legal Practitioners Involved in the Mining, Oil and Gas Industries" (30 Sept. 2008).

47   The system is elaborated in *Crown Minerals Act, S.S. 1984-85-86*, c. C-50.2; *Mineral Resources Act, 1985*, S.S. 1984-85-86, c. M-16.1; and Mineral Disposition Regulations, 1996, Sask. Reg. 30/86.

48   See the Petroleum and Natural Gas Regulation, 1969, Sask. Reg. 8/69, s. 43.5.g.i.

49   McAdam discusses this, *supra* note 46.

50   I am grateful to my colleague, legal scholar Marie-Ann Bowden, for discussions on this point.

51   *Cf. Seeking Common Ground: Roundtable Conference on First Nations and Métis Consultation and Accommodation: Conference Report* (Regina: Government of Saskatchewan Ministry of First Nations and Métis Relations, 2008): www.fnmr.gov.sk.ca/roundtable-conference-report.

52   *Lefthand, supra* note 3 at para. 40, per Slatter J.A.

53 *Little Salmon/Carmacks First Nation* v. *Yukon (Director, Agriculture Branch, Department of Energy, Mines & Resources)* 2008 YKCA 13, [2008] 4 C.N.L.R. 25 at para 95; leave to appeal to SCC granted 32850 (29 Jan. 2009).

54 *Lefthand, supra* note 3 at para. 45.

55 *Haida Nation, supra* note 1 at para. 53.

56 See, for example, *Hansard*, Standing Committee on Intergovernmental Affairs and Infrastructure No. 42 – Apr. 16, 2007 – 25th Legislature (Sask.) Vote 25.

57 *Hupacasath First Nation* v. *British Columbia (Minister of Forests)* 2005 BCSC 1712, 41 Admin L.R. (4th) 179 at para. 335.

58 *Dene Tha'* (Fed. Ct.) *supra* note 42 at paras. 133-34.

59 See also *Homalco Indian Band* v. *British Columbia (Minister of Agriculture, Food & Fisheries)* 2005 BCSC 283, 39 B.C.L.R. (4th) 263 at para. 108, temporarily restraining placement of further fish in a farming operation, until government fulfilled the duty to consult; and *Kruger Inc.* v. *Betsiamites First Nation*, 2006 QCCA 569, [2006] 3 C.N.L.R. 19, an injunction granted by a lower court resulting in delay in development until after a Court of Appeal decision; leave to appeal *Kruger Inc.* to SCC refused 384 N.R. 195 (20 Oct. 2005).

60 See, for example, *Frontenac Ventures Corp.* v *Ardoch Algonquin First Nation*, [2008] CarswellOnt 1168, 2008 CanLII 8247 (Ont. Sup Ct.), a company seeking an injunction when not able to carry out mining.

61 *Lefthand, supra* note 3 at para 38.

62 *Ahousaht Indian Band, supra* note 24.

63 *Ibid.*

64 *Paul First Nation, supra* note 37 at para. 7.

65 *Lefthand, supra* note 3 at para. 43. *Cf.* also *Douglas, supra* note 28 at para 45.

66 *Xats'ull First Nation* v. *Director, Environmental Management Act*, 2006-EMA-006(a) at para. 412: www.eab.gov.bc.ca/ema/2006ema006a.pdf.

67 Luke Simcoe, "Duty to consult should include funding: MNS," Saskatoon *StarPhoenix* (16 Mar. 2009) A3.

68 See, for example, *Hansard*, Standing Committee on Intergovernmental Affairs and Infrastructure No. 42- Apr. 16, 2007 – 25th Legislature (Sask.) Vote 25 (regarding Saskatchewan's program).

69 See *Red Chris Development Co.* v. *Quock*, 2006 BCSC 1472 at paras. 15-16, rejecting the claim of certain individuals who claimed they should have been consulted in addition to the elected leadership of the First Nation.

70   *Supra* note 22 at paras. 43-44, aff'd, *supra* note 23.

71   *Supra* note 23 at paras. 3, 5.

72   *Indian Act*, R.S.C. 1985, c. I-5.

73   Thomas Isaac, *Métis Rights* (Saskatoon: University of Saskatchewan Native Law Centre, 2008) at 41-48.

74   *Labrador Métis Nation* v. *Newfoundland and Labrador (Minister of Transportation and Works)*, *supra* note 26.

75   *Ibid.*, at para. 45.

76   *Ibid.*, at paras. 46-47.

77   *Ibid.*, at para. 52.

78   *Re Imperial Oil Resources Ventures Ltd.* [2007] A.E.U.B.D. No. 13.

79   *Ibid.*, at paras. 60-63.

80   The Métis Nation of Saskatchewan identified an instance in which a branch of the federal government was carrying on consultation with a committee appointed by the federal government as supposedly representative of Métis communities in the area: Thomas J. Bruner, "President of Métis Nation Demands Consultation," *Saskatchewan Sage: The Aboriginal Newspaper of Saskatchewan* (Mar. 2009) p. 3. Obviously, there is a legal error involved if the government seeks to consult with itself!

81   Jason Madden, general counsel for the Métis National Council, unpublished conference paper.

82   See *Tzeachten First Nation* v. *Canada (Attorney General)* 2007 BCCA 133, 281 D.L.R. (4th) 752, rev'g. *Tzeachten First Nation* v. *Canada (Attorney General)* 2006 BCSC 479, [2006] 6 W.W.R. 113.

83   See, for example, *Native Council of Nova Scotia*, *supra* note 23 at para. 89; *Labrador Métis Nation*, *supra* note 26 at para. 52; *Lefthand*, *supra* note 3 at para. 42.

84   *Haida Nation*, *supra* note 1 at para. 62, 63.

85   *Hupacasath First Nation* v. *British Columbia (Minister of Forests)* 2008 BCSC 1505, [2009] 1 C.N.L.R. 30 at para. 252.

86   *Ahousaht First Nation*, *supra* note 24 at para. 34; *Tzeachten First Nation*, *supra* note 82 at para. 24.

87   See, for example, *Hupacasath First Nation*, *supra* note 85 at paras. 180, 240.

88   *Supra* note 85.

89   *Ibid.*, at paras 42, 50.

90   *Kruger, supra* note 59 at paras. 47, 50.

91   *Lefthand, supra* note 3 at para. 165, per Conrad J.A.

92   *Hupacasath First Nation, supra* note 85 at paras. 255-56.

93   *Musqueam Indian Band* v. *Canada*, 2008 FCA 214, 297 D.L.R. (4th) 349 at paras. 45-46, 58, 297; leave to appeal to Supreme Court of Canada refused 32785 (4 Dec. 2008).

94   See *Frontenac, supra* note 60; *Platinex Inc.* v. *Kitchenuhmaykoosib Inninuwug First Nation*, [2008] 2 C.N.L.R. 301; varied by 2008 ONCA 533, [2008] 3 C.N.L.R. 302.

95   See *Hupacasath First Nation, supra* note 85 at paras. 231-32. *Cf. Musqueam Indian Band, supra* note 93 at paras. 48, 58.

96   *Cf. Haida Nation, supra* note 1 at para. 76.

97   *Dene Tha'* (Fed. Ct.), *supra* note 42 at para. 119. See also *Hupacasath First Nation, supra* note 85 at paras. 261-63.

98   *Dene Tha'* (Fed. Ct.), *supra* note 42 at paras. 133-34.

99   *Ka'a'gee Tu First Nation* v. *Canada (Minister of Indian & Northern Affairs)* 2007 FC 764, [2008] 2 F.C.R. 473 at paras. 73-75.

100 *Tsuu T'ina First Nation, supra* note 38 at paras. 38-43; see also the judgment of Conrad J.A. in *Lefthand, supra* note 3.

101 *Tsuu T'ina First Nation, supra* note 38 at 43-44.

102 See *Carrier Sekani Tribal Council, supra* note 2 at para. 56.

103 See especially *ibid, supra* note 2. See also *Kwikwetlem First Nation* v. *British Columbia (Utilities Commission)* 2009 BCCA 68 at paras. 8, 13-15. Although leave to appeal *Kwikwetlem* does not appear to have been sought, its future legal status may depend on the leave to appeal application in *Carrier Sekani, supra* note 2.

104 *Carrier Sekani, supra* note 2 at para. 14.

105 *Ibid.*, at para. 15. See also *Kwikwetlem First Nation, supra* note 103 at paras. 13-15.

106 See, for example, *Penelakut First Nation Elders* v. *British Columbia (Ministry of Water, Land and Air Protection)* [2004] B.C.E.A. No. 34 (B.C.E.A.B.) at paras. 147-48, 151-83.

107 A recent example is *Re SemCAMS Redwillow ULC* (Mar. 2009) 2009 LNCNEB 3, GH-2-2008 at para. 125 (N.E.B.).

Notes to Chapter Three

1   *Haida Nation* v. *British Columbia (Minister of Forests)* [2004] 3 S.C.R. 511, 2004 SCC 73 at para. 41.

2   See *Haida Nation, ibid.,* at paras. 43-45; *Taku River Tlingit First Nation* v. *British Columbia (Project Assessment Director)* [2004] 3 S.C.R. 550, 2004 SCC 74 at para. 32.

3   *Haida Nation, ibid.,* at para. 62.

4   *Ahousaht Indian Band* v. *Canada (Minister of Fisheries and Oceans)* 2008 FCA 112 at para. 54. See also *Saulteau First Nation* v. *British Columbia (Oil and Gas Commission)* 2004 BCCA 286 (adopting a reasonableness rather than a fiduciary standard on the Crown), leave to appeal to SCC refused 30463 (3 Mar. 2005).

5   *Haida Nation, supra* note 1 at para. 39.

6   *Mikisew Cree First Nation* v. *Canada (Minister of Canadian Heritage)* 2005 SCC 69, [2005] 3 S.C.R. 388 at para. 34.

7   *Haida Nation, supra* note 1 at para. 41.

8   *Ibid.,* at paras. 43-45.

9   *Ibid.,* at paras. 74, 77.

10 *Taku River Tlingit First Nation, supra* note 2.

11 *Ibid.,* at para. 31.

12 *Ibid.,* at paras. 33-46.

13 *Ibid.,* at paras. 40-41.

14 See, for example, Bernie J. Roth, "Meeting the Expectations for Public Consultation Under Guide 56"(1 Oct. 2002, Fraser Milner Casgrain): www.fmc-law.com/upload/en/publications/archive/2612107_MeetingExpectations_Bernie_Roth.pdf, at 7-8.

15 I am grateful to my colleague, Marie-Ann Bowden, at the University of Saskatchewan College of Law, for discussion on this issue.

16 See *Dene Tha' First Nation* v. *Canada (Minister of Environment)* 2006 FC 1354, [2007] 1 C.N.L.R. 1 [*Dene Tha'* (Fed. Ct.)] at para. 62 (deciding a public forum process was not sufficient to meet the requirements of consultation with the Dene Tha' First Nation), aff'd 2008 FCA 20, 378 N.R. 251.

17 See *Paul First Nation* v. *Parkland (County)* 2006 ABCA 128, 384 A.R. 366, at paras. 2-3, 7, 15. There would obviously be an exception giving rise to enhanced notice requirements if there were knowledge of specific Aboriginal rights affected.

18 *Haida Nation, supra* note 1 at para. 35.

19 *R. v. Douglas*, 2007 BCCA 265, 278 D.L.R. (4th) 263, at paras. 42-44; leave to appeal to SCC refused, 383 W.R. 382 (15 Nov. 2007).

20 *Metlakatla Indian Band v. Canada (Minister of Transport)* 2007 FC 553, 65 Admin. L.R. (4th) 152 at para. 29.

21 See *Douglas, supra* note 19 at para. 161 and *Ahousaht Indian Band, supra* note 4 at paras. 52-53.

22 *Xats'ull First Nation v. Director, Environmental Management Act*, 2006-EMA-006(a): www.eab.gov.bc.ca/ema/2006ema006a.pdf.

23 *Ibid.,* at paras. 275, 279.

24 *Ibid.,* at paras. 280-84, 302-304.

25 See, for example, *Musqueam Indian Band v. Canada*, 2008 FCA 214, [2008] 3 C.N.L.R. 29, at para. 8; leave to appeal to SCC refused 32785 (4. Dec. 2008).

26 *Hiawatha First Nation v. Ontario (Minister of Environment)* [2007] C.N.L.R. 186 at para. 60.

27 See, for example, W. Thomas Molloy & Brendan Delehanty, "The Evolving Duty of Consultation: Developing Relationships Between Business and First Nations" (Paper for Conference Board of Canada Council on Corporate Aboriginal Relations, 18-19 Sept. 2003): www.mlt.com/media/publications/WTMDutyToConsult.pdf; Tony Fogarassy, "Triggering the Duty of Consultation with Aboriginal Peoples" (Paper for Canadian Institute's 10th BC Gas Symposium, Vancouver, 6-7 Jun. 2007): www.cwilson.com/pubs/energy/dutyofconsultation.pdf.

28 *Little Salmon/Carmacks First Nation v. Yukon (Director, Agriculture Branch, Department of Energy, Mines & Resources)* 2008 YKCA 13, [2008] 4 C.N.L.R. 25; leave to appeal to SCC granted 32850 (29 Jan. 2008).

29 There have been a number of judgments in the ongoing dispute: [2006] 4 C.N.L.R. 152 (Ont. Sup. Ct. J.); [2007] 3 C.N.L.R. 181 (Ont. Sup. Ct. J.); [2007] 3 C.N.L.R. 221 (Ont. Sup. Ct. J.); and 2008 ONCA 533, dealing with contempt proceedings against members of the First Nation.

30 See, generally, *R. v. Lefthand*, 2007 ABCA 206, 77 Alta. L.R. (4th) 203 at paras. 162-69; leave to appeal to SCC refused 385 N.R. 392 (21 Feb. 2008). *Cf. Ka'a'gee Tu First Nation v. Canada (Minister of Indian & Northern Affairs)* 2007 FC 764, [2008] 2 F.C.R. 473 at para. 118 and Appendix B.

31 *Lefthand, ibid.*

32 *Haida Nation, supra note* 1 at paras. 43-45.

33   *Dene Tha'* (Fed. Ct.), *supra* note 16.

34   *Ka'a'gee Tu First Nation, supra* note 30.

35   See, for example, *Dene Tha'* (Fed. Ct.), *supra* note 16 at paras. 113, 114, 121; see also *Kwikwetlem First Nation* v. *British Columbia (Utilities Commission)* 2009 BCCA 68 at para. 70.

36   *Dene Tha'* (Fed. Ct.), *supra* note 16 at para. 116. *Cf.* also *Little Salmon/Carmacks First Nation, supra* note 28 at para. 33.

37   Government of Saskatchewan, Draft First Nations and Métis Consultation Policy Framework (Dec. 2008) at 8: www.fnmr.gov.sk.ca/adx/aspx/adxGetM edia.aspx?DocID=1932,1548,81,1,Documents&MediaID=806&Filename=Dr aftFramework-Dec2008.pdf.

38   *Ibid.*

39   *Cf. Mikisew Cree First Nation, supra* note 6 at paras. 55-57, discussing the role of the seriousness of impact on the Aboriginal community as foremost in a treaty context.

40   *Brokenhead Ojibway Nation* v. *Canada (Attorney General)* 2009 FC 484.

41   *Ibid.,* at para. 20.

42   *Ibid.,* at para. 25.

43   *Ibid.,* at para. 23

44   *Ibid.,* at para. 26.

45   *Ibid.,* at para. 34.

46   *Ibid.,* at paras. 39-41.

47   *Ibid.,* at para. 30.

48   *Haida Nation, supra* note 1 at para. 47.

49   *Ibid.,* at para. 50.

50   *Haida Nation* provides that minimal guidance in *ibid.,* at para. 47.

51   *Dene Tha'* (Fed. Ct.), *supra* note 16 at para. 82.

52   *Wii'litswx* v. *British Columbia (Minister of Forests)* 2008 BCSC 1139, [2008] 4 C.N.L.R. 315, at para. 239.

53   See *Hupacasath First Nation* v. *British Columbia (Minister of Forests)* 2008 BCSC 1505, [2009] 1 C.N.L.R. 30 at paras. 231-32.

54   *Lameman and Beaver Lake Cree Nation* v. *Alberta and Canada,* Statement of Claim, Action No. 080306718 (14 May 2008) (Alta. Q.B.): www.beaverlakecreenation.ca/upload/documents/statementofclaim.pdf.

55 *Delgamuukw* v. *British Columbia* [1997] 3 S.C.R. 1010 at para. 111.

56 *Ibid.*, at para. 166.

57 See, for example, James Wood, "Resource Revenues Key: FSIN," Saskatoon *StarPhoenix* (27 Jan. 2009) A3.

58 *Musqueam Indian Band* v. *British Columbia (Minister of Sustainable Resource Management)* 2005 BCCA 128, 251 D.L.R. (4th) 717 at para. 98.

59 For one media discussion, see Konrad Yakabuski, "Hydro-Québec a Slow Learner on Native Rights," *Globe and Mail* (12 Mar. 2009) B2.

Notes to Chapter Four

1 Roscoe Pound, "Law in Books and Law in Action: Historical Causes of Divergence Between the Nominal and Actual Law" (1910) 44 *American Law Review* 12.

2 *Ibid.*, at 24.

3 *Haida Nation* v. *British Columbia (Minister of Forests)* [2004] 3 S.C.R. 511, 2004 SCC 73 at para. 51.

4 Alberta, *Alberta's First Nations Consultation Guidelines on Land Management and Resource Development* (Nov. 2007): www.aboriginal.alberta.ca/documents/ First_Nations_and_Metis_Relations/First_Nations_Consultation_ guidelines_LM_RD.pdf .

5 As noted, BC has had a provincial policy on consultation since 2002. More recently, the government negotiated the *New Relationship* document that commits to the development of new consultation frameworks: www.gov.bc.ca/arr/newrelationship/down/new_relationship.pdf.

6 Saskatchewan currently has the *Interim Guide for Consultation with First Nations and Métis People* (Jan. 2008): www.fnmr.gov.sk.ca/documents/policy/ consultguide.pdf. It is also moving forward on a draft policy framework, *First Nation and Métis Consultation Policy Framework: Draft* (Dec. 2008): www.fnmr.gov.sk.ca/adx/aspx/adxGetMedia.aspx?DocID=1932,1548,81,1,Do cuments&MediaID=806&Filename=DraftFramework-Dec2008.pdf.

7 Manitoba, *Provincial Policy for Consultation with Aboriginal Peoples* (Jul. 2007): www.gov.mb.ca/ana/pdf/draft_aboriginal_consultation_policy_and_ guidelines.pdf.

8 Ontario, *Draft Guidelines for Ministries on Consultation with Aboriginal Peoples Related to Aboriginal Rights and Treaty Rights* (Jun. 2006): www.abori ginalaffairs.gov.on.ca/english/policy/draftconsultjune2006.pdf.

9　Quebec, *Interim Guide for Consulting the Aboriginal Communities* (2006): www.autochtones.gouv.qc.ca/publications_documentation/publications/guide-interimaire_en.pdf.

10　Nova Scotia, *Province of Nova Scotia Consultation with the Mi'kmaq: Interim Consultation Policy* (Jun. 2007): gov.ns.ca/abor/Download.aspx?serverfn=/abor/files/drm/5dbaa705-e29c-4f6f-b4e9-4f160cab395c.pdf&downloadfn=Nova%20Scotia%20Interim%20Consultation%20Policy%20Jun.%201807.pdf&contenttype=.

11　Canada, *Aboriginal Consultation and Accommodation – Interim Guidelines for Federal Officials to Fulfill the Duty to Consult*: www.ainc-inac.gc.ca/mr/is/acp/intgui-eng.pdf.

12　See *Hansard*, Standing Committee on Intergovernmental Affairs and Infrastructure No. 42 (16 Apr. 2007) – 25th Legislature (Sask.) Vote 25.

13　*Seeking Common Ground: Roundtable Conference on First Nations and Métis Consultation and Accommodation: Conference Report* (Regina: Government of Saskatchewan Ministry of First Nations and Métis Relations, 2008): www.fnmr.gov.sk.ca/roundtable-conference-report.

14　Saskatchewan, *First Nation and Métis Consultation Policy Framework: Draft* (Dec. 2008) *supra* note 6.

15　See also Warren Goulding, "Duty to Consult Process Rocky Despite Province's Optimism" (Apr. 2009) 12:4 *Eagle Feather News* 9.

16　Saskatchewan, Ministry of the Environment, *Operational Procedures for Consultations with First Nations and Métis Communities* (2007).

17　Canada, National Energy Board, *Consideration of Aboriginal Concerns in National Energy Board Decisions* (Jul. 2008): www.neb-one.gc.ca/clf-nsi/rthnb/nvlvngthpblc/brgnlppl/brgnlppl-eng.html.

18　Ontario Energy Board, *Aboriginal Consultation Policy*, EB-2007-0617 (Jun. 2007): www.oeb.gov.on.ca/documents/cases/EB-2007-0617/acp_policy_20070618.PDF.

19　See *ibid.*, at Appendix A.

20　Ontario, *Draft Guidelines for Ministries on Consultation with Aboriginal Peoples Related to Aboriginal Rights and Treaty Rights* (Jun. 2006), *supra* note 8 at 16.

21　*Ibid.*

22　See *ibid.* and Alberta, *Alberta's First Nations Consultation Guidelines on Land Management and Resource Development* (Nov. 2007), *supra* note 4 at 3-4.

23 See, for example, Manitoba, *Provincial Policy for Consultation with Aboriginal Peoples*, *supra* note 7 and Saskatchewan, *First Nation and Métis Consultation Policy Framework: Draft* (Dec. 2008), *supra* note 6.

24 See, for example, *Re Hydro One Networks Inc.*, EB-2007-0050 (2008): www.oeb.gov.on.ca/OEB/_Documents/EB-2007-0050/dec_HONI_ BruceMilton_20080915.pdf. The argument of the intervenor Métis Nation of Ontario is at www.oeb.gov.on.ca/documents/cases/EB-2007-0050/ intervenor_arguments/sub_metisnation_20080704.pdf.

25 *Re TransCanada Keystone Pipeline GP Ltd.* (Sept. 2007) 2007 LNCNEB 9, OH-1-2007 at para. 155 (N.E.B.).

26 *Re Enbridge Pipelines Inc.* (Feb. 2008) 2008 LNCNEB 2, OH-4-2007 (N.E.B.).

27 *Ibid.*, at para. 15, which lists Aboriginal parties that provided input during the hearing.

28 *Ibid.*, at para. 118, which sets out a number of intervenors at a later hearing.

29 *Ibid.*, at para. 30.

30 *Ibid.*, at para. 50.

31 *Ibid.*, at para. 150.

32 *Re SemCAMS Redwillow ULC* (Mar. 2009) 2009 LNCNEB 3, No. GH-2-2008 (N.E.B.).

33 *Ibid.*, at para. 125.

34 British Columbia, Utilities Commission, *First Nations Consultation in Proceedings Before the British Columbia Utilities Commission* (2007): www.bcuc.com/Documents/Proceedings/2007/DOC_17239_C12-22_First-Nations-Consultation-referencedoc.pdf.

35 British Columbia, Ministry of the Environment, Integrated Pest Management, *Draft Guidelines for IPM Proponents Conducting Consultations with First Nations* (2006): www.env.gov.bc.ca/epd/ipmp/first_nations_cons_guide/draft_guide.htm.

36 This is definitively required after *Carrier Sekani Tribal Council v. British Columbia (Utilities Commission)* 2009 BCCA 67, which provides a survey of past treatment of the duty to consult by administrative boards and tribunals, some of which took up the task willingly but some of which had been reluctant to undertake it.

37 British Columbia, *The New Relationship*, *supra* note 5.

38 See *Mining Amendment Act, 2009*, Bill 173, 39th parl., 1st sess: www.ontla.on.ca/ bills/bills-files/39_Parliament/Session1/b173.pdf. For some of the background discussion, see Ontario, Ministry of Northern Development and Mines, *Modernizing Ontario's Mining Act: Finding a Balance Discussion Paper* (Aug. 2008): www.mndm.gov.on.ca/miningact/pdf/discussion_paper_e.pdf.

39 See Assembly of First Nations, Special Chiefs Assembly, Res. No. 59/2005 (Dec. 2005): afn.ca/article.asp?id=2079. This was reasserted by then-National Chief Phil Fontaine before a Senate committee: Testimony on Bill C-292, Proceedings of Standing Senate Committee on Aboriginal Peoples, Issue 11 – Evidence – Apr. 16, 2008.

40 For an analysis of these more complex dynamics, see, for example, Joe Sawchuk, *The Dynamics of Native Politics: The Alberta Métis Experience* (Saskatoon: Purich, 1998).

41 *Labrador Métis Nation* v. *Newfoundland and Labrador (Minister of Transportation and Works)* 2007 NLCA 75, 288 D.L.R. (4th) 641; leave to appeal to SCC refused 32468 (29 May 2008).

42 *Cf. Ibid.*, at paras. 46-47.

43 See, for example, Assembly of First Nations, Special Chiefs Assembly, Res. No. 42/2007, "Denunciation of the Congress of Aboriginal Peoples" (Dec. 2007): www.afn.ca/article.asp?id=4071.

44 *"Newfoundland* & *Labrador* v. *Labrador Métis Nation:* Ground-breaking case for CAP" (Spring 2009) *The Forgotten People* [Congress of Aboriginal Peoples Newsletter] at 10-11: www.abo-peoples.org/media/people.pdf.

45 See Federation of Saskatchewan Indian Nations (FSIN), Lands & Resources, "Duty to Consult and Accommodate": www.fsin.com/ landsandresources/dutytoconsult.html. The paper describes early discussions with the government in the immediate wake of the *Haida Nation* decision through to the adoption of resolutions by the FSIN and the adoption of an FSIN consultation policy: www.fsin.com/legislativeassembly/downloads/ ConsultationPolicy.pdf.

46 *Seeking Common Ground: Roundtable Conference on First Nations and Métis Consultation and Accommodation: Conference Report, supra* note 13 at 5, 6, 18 and 19.

47 See Saskatchewan, *First Nation and Métis Consultation Policy Framework: Draft* (Dec. 2008), *supra* note 6.

48 See *Re Enbridge Pipelines Inc.*, supra note 26 at paras. 127-31.

49 Alberta, *Alberta's First Nations Consultation Guidelines on Land Management and Resource Development, supra* note 4.

50   See, for example, *Re Enbridge Pipelines Inc.*, *supra* note 26 at paras. 132, 143. In this latter example, however, the Métis Nation of Saskatchewan had difficulty identifying potential impacts of the project, due to the absence of a Métis traditional land use survey.

51   See metisbarefacts.blogspot.com/2008/04/duty-to-consult-alberta.html, as well as www.albertametis.com/MNAHome/News-Archive/Metis-Rights-and-the-Duty-to-Consult-and-Accommoda.aspx.

52   Métis Nation of Alberta, *Consultation Policy Package* (Jul. 2008): www.alberta-metis.ca/getdoc/fbf6af78-76fd-44b2-80f1-f0018029ce45/MNA_Con-sultation_Policy_Package_July_2008.aspx.

53   Métis Nation of Ontario, *Towards a Consultation Framework for Ontario Métis – 2007/08 Community Consultations: What We Heard Report* (Jul. 2008): www.metisnation.org/consultations/framework_final_report.pdf. See also *Métis Consultation and Accommodation: A Guide for Government & Industry on Engaging Métis in Ontario*: www.metisnation.org/consultations/PDF/Duty_to_Consult_Guide.pdf, offering several prescriptions to government and industry on how to consult with Métis communities in Ontario.

54   Robert Lafontaine, "Saskatchewan Métis Concerned About Duty to Consult" (Apr. 2009) 12:4 *Eagle Feather News* 11.

55   *Ibid.*

56   On at least an interim basis, the Métis Nation of Saskatchewan has offered its *Statement of Principles on Métis Consultation and Accommodation* (May 2008): www.mn-s.ca/pdfs/Statement%20of%20Principles.pdf.

57   For a summary of Métis governance structures, see Jason Madden, "The Métis Nation's Self-Government Agenda: Issues and Options for the Future," in Frederica Wilson & Melanie Mallet, *Métis-Crown Relations: Rights, Identity, Jurisdiction, and Governance* (Toronto: Irwin Law, 2008), p. 323. For historical background on the situation of the Métis in Canada, see Donald Purich, *The Metis* (Toronto: James Lorimer, 1988).

58   See Métis Nation of Ontario: www.metisnation.org/consultations; see also Métis Nation British Columbia, *Consultation Guidelines* (Feb. 2009): www.mpcbc.bc.ca/pdf/Final%20Consultation%20Guidelines.pdf.

59   Northern Secwepemc te Qelmucw (NStQ), *Consultation and Accommodation Guidelines for Government and Third Parties*, 1st edition (Jun. 2003). As of June 2009, the Northern Shuswap have released a new edition of their consultation guidelines: *2009 NStQ Consultation Guidelines: A Guide for Government and Third Parties* (2009): www.nstq.org/Natural%20Resources/2009%20Northern%20Secwepemc%20te%20Qelmucw%20Consultation%20Guidelines.pdf.

60 Horse Lake First Nation Consultation Policy: www.horselakefirstnation.co m/consultation-policy.html.

61 *Ibid.*

62 Thunderchild First Nation, "Duty to Consult Report": www.thunderchild.ca/ default.aspx?ID=Duty%20to%20consult.

63 Ontario, *Draft Guidelines for Ministries on Consultation with Aboriginal Peoples Related to Aboriginal Rights and Treaty Rights* (Jun. 2006), *supra* note 8 at 16-17.

64 *Xats'ull First Nation* v. *Director, Environmental Management Act*, 2006-EMA-006(a) at para. 412: www.eab.gov.bc.ca/ema/2006emao06a.pdf.

65 *Ibid.*, at paras. 369-376, 392, 411.

66 A number of corporate filings have referred to the potential impacts on their financial statements of the duty to consult. See: *Starfield Resources Inc. Annual Information Form* (29 Feb. 2008): www.sec.gov/Archives/edgar/ data/1074795/000095013308002953/w65774e2ovf.htm; *Oilsands Quest Inc. Annual Information Form* (30 Apr. 2008): www.sec.gov/Archives/edgar/ data/1096791/000103570408000299/d58004e10vk.htm; *Cameco Corporation Annual Information Form* (Mar. 28, 2008): www.sec.gov/Archives/edgar/ data/1009001/000113031908000282/039572exv99w1.htm; *Fording Canadian Coal Trust Annual Information Form* (Mar. 14, 2008): www.sec.gov/Archives/ edgar/data/1158113/000136231008001452/c72727exv99wa.htm; and *Talisman Energy Corporate Responsibility Report 2006*: www.sec.gov/Archives/edgar/ data/201283/000110465907023381/a07-8413_1ex99d2.htm.

67 *Talisman Energy Corporate Responsibility Report 2006, ibid.*

68 Natasha Affolder, "Is International Law an Effective Eco-Lobbying Tool?" (2009) Am. Soc. Int'l L. Proc. (forthcoming).

69 Saskatchewan, Ministry of the Environment, *Mineral Exploration Guidelines for Saskatchewan* (Nov. 2007): www.environment.gov.sk.ca/adx/aspx/adxGe tMedia.aspx?DocID=1512,803,531,94,88,Documents&MediaID=754&Filena me=Mineral+Exploration+Guidelines.pdf.

70 Natural Resources Canada, *Mining Information Kit for Aboriginal Communities* (2006): www.pdac.ca/pdac/advocacy/aboriginal-affairs/2006-mining-toolkit-eng.pdf.

71 Mining Association of Canada, *Towards Sustainable Mining Guiding Principles: Draft Framework for Mining and Aboriginal Peoples* (Dec. 2006): www.mining.ca/www/media_lib/TSM_Documents/2006_Protocols/ Draft_Aboriginal_Framework_Final.pdf.

72 Saskatchewan Mining Association, Best Management Practice 14 (May 2007): www.er.gov.sk.ca/default.aspx?DN=10ac9797-bdb3-4456-9028-69ccd9b7db88.

73 Joe Friesen, "Asian Investors Back Natives Bands: Hedge Fund Focused on Developing Aboriginal Land Popular in China, Korea," *Globe & Mail* (9 Mar. 2009) A5.

74 See *Re Enbridge Pipelines Inc.*, *supra* note 26 at paras. 119-24, detailing the identification of potentially affected groups through the use of a 160 km consultation corridor. See also *Re TransCanada Keystone Pipeline GP Ltd.*, *supra* note 25 at para. 127, detailing the identification of potentially affected groups within a 50 km corridor.

75 Matt Goerzen, "Pipeline firm strikes deal with Man. First Nations," Saskatoon *StarPhoenix* (13 Jan. 2009) A5.

76 *Ibid.* The National Energy Board decision on Enbridge's application noted these First Nations' support for the project following Enbridge's Aboriginal engagement efforts: *Re Enbridge Pipelines Inc.*, *supra* note 26.

77 See Joe Friesen, "Dispute Shuts Alberta Clipper Pipeline," *Globe & Mail* (1 Oct. 2008) A6; Barb Pacholik, "Company, First Nations hold meeting," Saskatoon *StarPhoenix* (30 Sept. 2008) A11.

78 James Wood & Lana Haight "Pipeline Company, First Nations reach 'new alliance'" Saskatoon *StarPhoenix* (4 Oct. 2008) A3.

79 *Ibid.*

80 For examples from SEC filings, see filings by: *Starfield Resources Inc.*: www.sec.gov/Archives/edgar/data/1074795/000095013308002953/w657 74e2ovf.htm at p. 6; *Oilsands Quest Inc.*: www.sec.gov/Archives/edgar/data/1096791/000103570408000299/d58004e1ovk.htm at p. 29; Cameco: www.sec.gov/Archives/edgar/data/1009001/000113031908000282/039572exv99w1.htm; *Fording Canadian Coal Trust*: www.sec.gov/Archives/edgar/data/1158113/000136231008001452/c72727exv99wa.htm at p. 34.

81 See Craig Jackson & Michael Bray, "Financial, Accounting and Auditing Implications," in Bryan Horrigan & Simon Young (Eds.), *Commercial Implications of Native Title* (Sydney: Federation Press, 1997), p. 200; and Bryan Horrigan, "Practical Implications for Financiers, Land Dealers, Investors and Professional Advisers," in *ibid.*, p. 215.

82 *Supra* note 80.

83 See David Ebner, "Investor Urges Enbridge to Assess Risk of Delay," *Globe & Mail* (30 Mar. 2009) B1.

84   Alberta, *Alberta's First Nations Consultation Guidelines on Land Management and Resource Development*, *supra* note 4 at 3.

85   *Ibid.*, at 5.

86   See, for example, *Horse Lake First Nation Consultation Policy*, *supra* note 60, ss. 12-13. See also Robert Talbot, *Negotiating the Numbered Treaties: An Intellectual and Political Biography of Alexander Morris* (Saskatoon: Purich, 2009), especially pp. 70, 147, 157, and 175 for a historical perspective on First Nations' consultation policies. In refusing to consult with anyone other than government or the lead proponents, present-day First Nations are being entirely consistent with the practices of their ancestors.

87   See *Re Enbridge Pipelines Inc.*, *supra* note 26 at paras. 119ff, discussing Enbridge's Indigenous Peoples Policy; *Re TransCanada Keystone Pipeline GP Ltd.*, *supra* note 25 at paras. 127ff, referring to TransCanada's Aboriginal Relations Policy; and *Re SemCAMS Redwillow ULC*, *supra* note 32 at paras. 91ff, discussing the SemCAMS Aboriginal Engagement Guidelines and Consultation Protocols.

88   David Szablowski, *Transnational Law and Local Struggles: Mining, Communities, and the World Bank* (Oxford: Hart, 2007).

89   *Ibid.*, at 292.

90   *Ibid.*, at 289-305.

91   Pound, *supra* note 1 at 36.

Notes to Chapter Five

1   For seminal international law writings on the rights of Indigenous peoples, see S. James Anaya, *Indigenous Peoples in International Law*, 2nd Edition (Oxford: Oxford University Press, 2004); Russel Lawrence Barsh, "Indigenous Peoples: An Emerging Object of International Law" (1986) 80 Am. J. Int'l L. 369; Siegfried Wiessner, "Rights and Status of Indigenous Peoples: A Global Comparative and International Legal Analysis" (1999) 12 Harv. Hum. Rts. J. 57; and Benedict Kingsbury, "Reconciling Five Competing Conceptual Structures of Indigenous Peoples' Claims in International and Comparative Law" (2001) 34 N.Y.U.J. Int'l L. & Pol. 189.

2   Early in Chapter 1, the roles of "fit" and "soundness" were discussed as important elements in testing the application of different theoretical approaches, following Ronald Dworkin's *Law's Empire* (Cambridge: Belknap, 1986).

3   For an interesting recent discussion, see James (Sa'ke'j) Youngblood Henderson, *Indigenous Diplomacy and the Rights of Peoples: Achieving UN Recognition* (Saskatoon: Purich, 2008).

4   *United Nations Declaration on the Rights of Indigenous Peoples*, U.N.G.A. Res. 61/295, U.N. Doc. A/RES/61/295 (13 Sept. 2007) (2007) 46 I.L.M. 1013.

5   For a discussion of the complex dynamics of the last-minute efforts to bring African states onside, see Dwight Newman, "The Law and Politics of Indigenous Rights in the Postcolonial African State" (2009) Am. Soc. Int'l L. Proceedings (forthcoming).

6   UN media release, "General Assembly Adopts Declaration on Rights of Indigenous Peoples; 'Major Step Forward' Towards Human Rights For All, Says President," U.N. Doc GA/10612 (13 Sept. 2007): www.un.org/News/Press/docs/2007/ga10612.doc.htm.

7   See Newman, *supra* note 5 for the background to this claim.

8   *Supra* note 6.

9   See Jenny Macklin, Minister of Indigenous Affairs, "Statement on the United Nations Declaration on the Rights of Indigenous Peoples" (3 April 2009): www.un.org/esa/socdev/unpfii/documents/Australia_official_statement_endorsement_UNDRIP.pdf.

10 www.radionz.co.nz/news/stories/2009/05/17/1245b0225af1.

11 International Labour Organization (ILO) Convention Concerning Indigenous and Tribal Peoples in Independent Countries (ILO No. 169) (1989) 72 ILO Official Bull. 59, entered into force Sept. 5, 1991.

12 *Ibid.*

13 *Supra* note 6.

14 Anaya, *Indigenous Peoples in International Law*, *supra* note 1.

15 *Ibid.*, 155. The texts of the *Draft Declaration* of 1994 and the final *Declaration* of 2007 refer in their later forms to a requirement of free, prior, and informed consent for legislative and administrative decisions that affect Aboriginal communities, differing from the wording in Article 6 of the ILO Convention, which had referred to efforts to attain agreement. This represents a certain hardening of the wording of the consultation requirements. The texts of the *Draft* and final *Declaration* on consultation in the context of resource development similarly refer to free, prior, and informed consent before resource development can proceed, whereas Article 15(2) of the ILO Convention had referred to efforts to attain agreement, participation in the economic activity, and compensation for damage resulting, again reflecting a hardening of the wording.

16 See Assembly of First Nations Resolution No. 22 (2008): www.afn.ca/article.asp?id=4285. See also British Columbia Assembly of First Nations 4th Annual Regional Chiefs' Special Assembly Res. No. 17/2008 (Feb. 2008): www.bcafn.ca/index.php?option=com_docman&task=doc_view&gid=371.

17 One example appears in Canada's Statement on Examples of Applications of the Principle of Free, Prior, and Informed Consent (FPIC) at the National and International Levels (Geneva, July 2005): www.ainc-inac.gc.ca/ap/ia/stmt/unp/05/pop/anx-eng.asp.

18 See *Mitchell* v. *Canada (M.N.R.)* [2001] 1 S.C.R. 911, 2001 SCC 33 at para. 81.

19 *Haida Nation* v. *British Columbia (Minister of Forests)* [2004] 3 S.C.R. 511, 2004 SCC 73 at para. 46. The reference is to *A Guide for Consultation with Maori* (Wellington: Ministry of Justice, 1997): www.justice.govt.nz/pubs/reports/1998/maori_consultation/index.html.

20 Daniel Guttman, "Australian and Canadian Approaches to Native Title Pre-Proof," [2005] Australian Indigenous Law Reporter 39: www.austlii.edu.au/au/journals/AILR/2005/39.html.

21 *Mabo and Others* v. *Queensland (No. 2)* [1992] HCA 23, (1992) 175 C.L.R. 1.

22 See Peter H. Russell, *Recognizing Aboriginal Title: The Mabo Case and Indigenous Resistance to English-Settler Colonialism* (Toronto: University of Toronto Press, 2005).

23 *Mabo and Others* v. *Queensland (No. 2), supra* note 21.

24 See Melissa Perry & Stephen Lloyd, *Australian Native Title Law* (Sydney: Lawbook, 2003).

25 *Wik Peoples* v. *Queensland* (1996) 187 CLR 1.

26 *Native Title Amendment Act, 1998* (Aust. Cth.).

27 *Native Title Act, 1993* (Aust. Cth.): sections 26-30 provide much of the framework.

28 *Ibid.*, ss. 35-36.

29 See *Native Title (Queensland) State Provisions Amendment Act (No 2) 1998* (Queensland); *Native Title State Provisions Act, 1999* (Queensland); and *Native Title Resolution Act, 2000* (Queensland). See also Kathrine Morgan-Wicks, "Balancing Native Title and Mining Interests: The Queensland Experience," in Christopher J.F. Boge (Ed.), *Justice for All? Native Title in the Australian Legal System* (Brisbane: Lawyers Books Publications, 2001) p. 65.

30 See Morgan-Wicks, *ibid.*, at 68, 71-79.

31 *Ibid.*, at 76, comparing s. 658 of the amended Queensland *Mineral Resources Act, 1989* with s. 30A of the national *Native Title Act*.

32 *Ibid.*, at 74, 76, 84. An additional efficiency is gained by this tribunal hav-
    ing simultaneous jurisdiction in relation to the right to negotiate issues
    along with cultural heritage objects issues. Challenges obviously arise if this
    Tribunal becomes backlogged.

33 The *Constitution Act, 1867* had added to its division of powers provisions the
    provincial resources jurisdiction in s. 92A.

34 *Ibid.*, s. 91(24) grants jurisdiction to the federal government over legislation
    related to "Indians, and Lands reserved for the Indians."

35 *Native Title Act, 1993* (Aust. Cth.), *supra* note 27, s. 24. See also the discussion
    in Russell, *supra* note 22 at 371-75.

36 *Ibid.*, ss. 24BB, 24CB, 24DB.

37 See K.D. MacDonald, "Commercial Implications of Native Title for Mining
    and Resources," in Bryan Horrigan & Simon Young (Eds.), *Commercial
    Implications of Native Title* (Sydney: Federation Press, 1997), pp. 122-23.

38 See *Native Title Act, 1993* (Aust. Cth.), *supra* note 27 at ss. 33, 33(2). These
    sections imply that profit-sharing can be developed in negotiated resolutions
    but cannot be imposed through arbitration.

39 MacDonald, *supra* note 37 at 123.

40 *Ibid.*

INDEX

British Columbia Supreme Court 35, 42

British Columbia Utilities Commission 69

Brokenhead Ojibway Nation v. *Canada: Keystone Pipeline* 57

C

Canadian Nuclear Safety Commission 38

Carrier Sekani Tribal Council v. *British Columbia* 11, 105n103; as to administrative decision-making boards and tribunals 111n36

Charter of Rights: engagement of 25

common law 14, 23, 80, 95

compensation 61, 77; in Australia 91; in UN *Draft Declaration* 85; economic 61-3, 69, 73, 77; in ILO Convention 84, for irreversible breach 61-2; non-compensable damage 49; retroactive 62; other forms of 63

Congress of Aboriginal Peoples (CAP) 40, 70-1

Constitution Act, 1867 119n33-4

Constitution Act, 1982 9, 14, 89; s. 35 9-10, 15, 22; as dynamic 20

consultation: "good consultation" 46-7, 59, 63-4; meaningful 48, 54-5, 63-4; "meaningful record" to establish consultation 42; reasonable efforts to consult 41, 44, 47, 51, 55, 68

consultation partners 35-40, 44-5, 54-5; Aboriginal partners *which see*; consultation corridor 76; explicitness necessary 36; identifying 38-40; Métis 39-40, 70, 71, 72

consultation policies. *See under* Aboriginal; corporate; government; Métis.

content of duty to consult 47-59; based on strength of Aboriginal claim and seriousness of impact 50; intensity matrix 56; spectrum 46, 48-9, 50. *See also* adverse impact; *prima facie* strength of claim; seriousness of effect.

corporate consultation policies 10, 74-7; in mining sector 75; policy interactions amounting to "law" 78-9; corporate consultation practices 76-7

corporate involvement in law-making processes 75, 79, 81

Crown: constitutional duty to consult 9-10, 15-17, 21, 32, 36-7, 41, 44, 51-5, 58-9; in *Haida* case *which see*; honour of *which see*; option to include third parties 35, 36, 43, 90; sovereignty 19-20

D

Dakota: and corporate negotiation 76; Dakota Sioux and Aboriginal title claim 56

Declaration on the Rights of Indigenous Peoples (UN 2007) 82-3, 85-7; Aboriginal veto power 86; Article 20 84; Article 30 84-5; Canada voted against 82, 86; *Draft Declaration* (1994) 83, 84-5, 87; "free, prior, and informed consent" (FPIC) 85-6, 87

Delgamuukw case: Aboriginal rights 62 (note 55); Australian interest in 88

E

F

G

government consultation policies 36, 55-6, 70; provincial 66-8, 69, 89; and industry stakeholders 68

H

Haida Nation 9, 12-13, 17; not consulted prior to government action 3, 49

Haida Nation v. *British Columbia* 19, 20, 23, 32, 42; and accommodation 48, 59-60; Crown duty to consult 12, 16-17, 19, 23, 25-7, 30, 35, 48-9; as departure from earlier case law 10, 30, 43; interlocutory injunctions 17-18; and provincial policy 66; triggering test 25, 27-8, 29, 48

Haida Nation trilogy 9-11, 12-14, 15, 72

Halfway River First Nation v. *British Columbia:* early lower court recognition of duty to consult 10 (note 10)

Hiawatha First Nation v. *Ontario* 52

honour of the Crown 12-13, 15, 16-17, 25, 30, 47, 49, 54, 94; cannot be delegated 35, 90

Horse Lake First Nation (HLFN): consultation model independent of government funding 73; consultation policy 72-3; refusal to accept consultation with other than government or the lead proponents 78 (note 86)

Hupacasath First Nation v. *British Columbia* 35, 42; and compensation 61 (note 53); influenced by *Tsilhqot'in Nation* case 100n44

I

Indian Act 39, 71

injunctions 16, 35, 42-3, 53, 94; interlocutory 17-18

international law 74-5, 79, 91-2, 93-4; and duty to consult 81-2, 82-8. *See also* Australia; International Labour Organization; United Nations.

International Labour Organization (ILO): ILO Convention No. 169 (1989) 83-4, 86; Article 6 (government obligations) 83-4; Article 15(2) (resources) 84

international perspectives 81-92

J

judicial intervention 34, 41-4, 88, 94; damages 43; provincial superior court vs Federal Court jurisdiction 41, 89. *See also* injunctions; litigation; remedies.

justification test: in *Sparrow* 9, 43

K

Ka'a'gee Tu First Nation v. *Canada* 43 (note 99), 54-5; irreversible effects of government action 53 (note 30)

Kitchenuhmaykoosib Inninuwug First Nation 42-3. *See further* Platinex Inc.

knowledge element of duty to consult trigger 12, 16, 25-9, 34, 48, 50; constructive 25, 26, 27; necessity for "meaningful knowledge" 28-9, 34

Kruger Inc. v. *Betsiamites First Nation* 41 (note 90), 103n59

Kwikwetlem First Nation v. *British Columbia:* administrative boards and tribunals 44 (note 103); meaningful consultation 55 (note 35)

L

Labrador Métis Nation v. *Newfoundland and Labrador* 39-40, 70

"law in action" *v.* "law in books" 65-6, 77, 80, 93-4

litigation 26, 34, 52, 60

Little Salmon/Carmacks First Nation v. *Yukon* 11, 52, 96n7

lower courts: creation of legislation outside application of duty to consult 31; on municipalities 30-1; on government action 30-2; inconsistent with *Haida Nation* jurisprudence 30; limiting duty to consult trigger 28, 29-30; limits/constraints 44-5, 51-3; recognizing duty to consult 10, 21-2, 23-4, 44-5; and privately owned lands 21. *See also* Supreme Court.

M

Mabo and Others v. *Queensland* 88

MacKenzie Gas Pipeline. See *Dene Tha'* and *Brokenhead Ojibway*

McLachlin, C.J.C. (*Haida Nation* case) 12-13, 16, 17, 23, 25, 28, 35, 44, 48, 53, 59, 87

Metlakatla Indian Band v. *Canada:* reasonable consultation 51 (note 20)

Métis consultation policies 70-72

Métis Nation of Saskatchewan 38, 72, 104 (note 80); other provincial Métis Nation organizations' consultation frameworks 72

Mikisew Cree First Nation v. *Canada* 9, 13; and treaty rights 13, 25, 27, 28, 48, 108 (note 39)

mineral/resource extraction 33, 74, 75, 84, 89

Mining Amendment Act, 2009 (Ont) 70 (note 38)

Mining Association of Canada 75

Ministry of Energy and Resources: Sask 33

Ministry of the Environment: BC 69; Sask 67-8

Mitchell v. *Canada:* example of *Draft Declaration* provisions referred to in case law 87 (note 18)

municipalities not to consult 30

Musqueam Indian Band v. *Canada* 42 (note 93), 52 (note 25), 61 (note 58)

N

nation-to-nation: discussions between Aboriginal and Asian nations 76; relationships 41

National Energy Board 57-9, 67, 68-9, 76

National Native Title Tribunal (Australia) 89

Native Council of Nova Scotia 28, 38-9, 40

Native Title Act, 1993 (Australia) subs. 25(2) 88

Re TransCanada Keystone Pipelines: corporate policy interacting with government decision-making processes 79 (note 87)

reconciliation 25, 30, 40, 47, 49, 54, 59-60, 63-4, 94; as result vs process 19, 20-1

Recognition and Reconciliation Act (BC) 69

relationship: duty to consult as fostering 44, 47, 94; consultation relationships in legislation 69

remedies: judicial 42-5; remedy for failure of duty to consult distinct from other breaches 43

reserve land 13, 26

resource development 19, 32, 91; in Australia 90-1; duty to consult impact on 10, 50, 57, 74

resource / mineral extraction 33, 74, 75, 84, 89

results-oriented theoretical approach 19, 21

revenue-sharing 61, 62

"Right to Negotiate" (Australia) 87-9, 90

S

Saulteau First Nation v. *British Columbia:* "reasonable efforts" 47 (note 4)

Saskatchewan: consultation context v. British Columbia 56, 62; consultation policy framework 36, 56, 66-7, 71-2, 73; funding available for consultation process 38; permit-by-

permit process 33; resource rights 32-3, 75; and treaty rights 62

Saskatchewan Mineral Exploration and Government Advisory Committee guidelines 75

Saskatchewan Mining Association policy document 75

scope of duty to consult 16, 20, 28, 46-59, 62; dependant on scope of Aboriginal rights 26-7, 51-3. *See also* content.

seriousness of effect: as element of duty to consult spectrum 12-13, 16, 18, 48-9, 50, 53, 56

"sharp dealing" 16-17

strength of claim. *See prima facie* strength of claim.

Supreme Court of Canada 10-14, 26-30, 35, 38, 54, 59, 66; case law 23, 32, 48-9, 54; and UN *Draft Declaration* 87; leaving room for lower court interpretation of duty to consult 10, 15-16, 23-4, 44-5, 48, 70, 80-1, 93

T

Taku River Tlingit First Nation v. *British Columbia* 9, 13, 47 (note 2), 48, 49-50

Talisman Energy 74

third parties 37-8, 88; affected by failure to consult *which see*; not owing duty to consult 10, 13, 35-6

Thunderchild First Nation: consultation policy 73

Tlicho Agreement: consultation provisions 96n7

Dwight G. Newman is Associate Professor
of Law at the University of Saskatchewan,
where he served as Associate Dean of Law
from 2006 to 2009. He is also an Honourary
Senior Research Fellow at the University of
the Witwatersrand School of Law in South
Africa. He completed his law degree at the
University of Saskatchewan, following which
he served as a law clerk to Chief Justice Lamer
and Justice LeBel at the Supreme Court of
Canada. He completed his doctorate at Oxford
University, where he studied as a Rhodes Scholar
and as a SSHRC Doctoral Fellow. He has
written numerous articles on Aboriginal law,
constitutional law, and international law, and he
is co-author of *Understanding Property: A Guide
to Canada's Property Law,* 2nd edition.